ITEM RESPONSE THEORY

SERIES IN UNDERSTANDING STATISTICS

NATASHA BERETVAS   Series Editor-in-Chief
PATRICIA LEAVY   Qualitative Editor

Quantitative Statistics

Confirmatory Factor Analysis
Timothy J. Brown

Effect Sizes
Steve Olejnik

Exploratory Factor Analysis
Leandre Fabrigar and
Duane Wegener

Multilevel Modeling
Joop Hox

Structural Equation Modeling
Marilyn Thompson

Tests of Mediation
Keenan Pituch

Measurement

Item Response Theory
Christine DeMars

Reliability
Patrick Meyer

Validity
Catherine Taylor

Qualitative

Oral History
Patricia Leavy

The Fundamentals
Johnny Saldaña

CHRISTINE DeMARS

ITEM RESPONSE THEORY

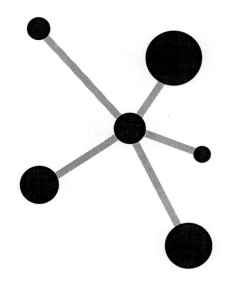

OXFORD
UNIVERSITY PRESS
2010

OXFORD
UNIVERSITY PRESS

Oxford University Press, Inc., publishes works that further Oxford University's
objective of excellence in research, scholarship, and education.

Oxford   New York
Auckland   Cape Town   Dar es Salaam   Hong Kong   Karachi
Kuala Lumpur   Madrid   Melbourne   Mexico City   Nairobi
New Delhi   Shanghai   Taipei   Toronto

With offices in
Argentina   Austria   Brazil   Chile   Czech Republic   France   Greece
Guatemala   Hungary   Italy   Japan   Poland   Portugal   Singapore
South Korea   Switzerland   Thailand   Turkey   Ukraine   Vietnam

Published by Oxford University Press, Inc.
198 Madison Avenue, New York, New York 10016

www.oup.com

Oxford is a registered trademark of Oxford University Press, Inc.

Library of Congress Cataloging-in-Publication Data
DeMars, Christine.
Item response theory / Christine DeMars.
p.   cm. — (Series in understanding statistics)
Includes bibliographical references.
ISBN 978-0-19-537703-3 (alk. paper)
1. Item response theory.   2. Psychometrics.   I. Title.
BF39.2.I84D46 2010
150.28′7—dc22
2009030941

Printed in the United States of America
on acid-free paper

TABLE OF CONTENTS

I TEM RESPONSE THEORY

1

INTRODUCTION

ITEM RESPONSE THEORY (IRT) models show the relationship between the ability or trait (symbolized θ) measured by the instrument and an item response. The item response may be *dichotomous* (two categories), such as right or wrong, yes or no, agree or disagree. Or, it may be *polytomous* (more than two categories), such as a rating from a judge or scorer or a Likert-type response scale on a survey. The construct measured by the items may be an academic proficiency or aptitude, or it may be an attitude or belief.

What do we use IRT for? One of the basic reasons is to score tests or surveys. The IRT score is often called an *ability, trait*, or *proficiency*. The IRT scoring takes into account the item difficulty and discrimination. Items that are more discriminating, or more reliable, are weighted more heavily, so IRT scores can be more reliable than number-correct scores. If different examinees take different tests, the IRT scores adjust for the difference in difficulty. This makes computer adaptive testing (CAT) possible. In CAT, the test items are selected to match each examinee's proficiency, so that the examinee will not be bored by easy items or frustrated by overly difficult items. The IRT scoring puts the scores from the different test forms onto the same metric, so that each examinee can have a customized test form. Item response theory also provides an index of the precision of the test score—the *standard error of measurement*—for each examinee.

Additionally, IRT can be used in test or scale development. Item response theory analysis supplies indices of item difficulty and discrimination. Knowing the item difficulty is useful when building tests to match the trait levels of a target population. For example, the items on a fourth grade science test should not be so easy that the average fourth-grader answers nearly all the items correctly, nor should they be so difficult that the average student answers nearly all of them incorrectly. Similarly, an instrument intended to measure well-being in a college population should not consist of items only endorsed by those with clinical depression. Another item index, *discrimination*, is useful for selecting items that differentiate well between examinees with low and high levels of the proficiency or attitude measured by the test items. Together, difficulty and discrimination can be used to calculate the standard error of measurement or reliability of the scores. These basic indices provided by IRT have analogs in classical test theory (CTT). The following sections describe both the IRT and CTT indices and how they are related. The IRT indices are more readily understood in the context of the formal mathematical models for describing the item response probabilities. These models are described later in the chapter; in the sections that immediately follow, the IRT indices are introduced only in general terms, leaving details for later.

Item Difficulty

Difficulty is defined in both CTT and IRT in terms of the likelihood of correct response, not in terms of the perceived difficulty or amount of effort required. In CTT, the difficulty index, P, is the proportion of examinees who answer the item correctly (sometimes P is called the P-value, but this terminology will be avoided here because it is easily confused with the p-value, or probability value, used in statistical hypothesis testing, which has an entirely different meaning). For polytomous items, the item difficulty is the mean score. So, counterintuitively, a more difficult item has a lower difficulty index in CTT.

In IRT, the difficulty index, b, is on the same metric as the proficiencies or traits. This metric is arbitrary, but often it is anchored such that the proficiency distribution in a designated group has a mean of 0 and standard deviation of 1. The item difficulty identifies the proficiency at which about 50% of the examinees (or a little more, depending on the model) are expected to answer the item correctly. For example, if $b = 0.2$, then about 50% of examinees with proficiency $= 0.2$ would get the item right. A larger percent of examinees with proficiency $= 0.5$ would get the item right. In contrast to CTT, difficult items have higher difficulty indices.

Item Discrimination

A higher discrimination means that the item differentiates (discriminates) between examinees with different levels of the construct. Thus, high discrimination is desirable. The purpose of using the instrument is to differentiate (discriminate) between examinees who know the material tested and those who do not, or on an attitude scale, between those who have positive attitudes and those who have negative attitudes. In CTT, the corrected item-total point-biserial correlation is the typical index of discrimination; when this is positive, examinees who answer the item correctly (or endorse the item) score higher on the sum of the remaining items than do those who answer the item incorrectly (or disagree with the item). In IRT, an index symbolized as a is a measure of the item discrimination. This index is sometimes called the *slope*, because it indicates how steeply the probability of correct response changes as the proficiency or trait increases. In both CTT and IRT, higher values indicate greater discrimination.

Reliability and Standard Error of Measurement

In CTT, reliability is generally defined as the ratio of true score variance to observed variance $\left(\frac{\sigma_T^2}{\sigma_X^2}\right)$, or the squared correlation between true and observed scores $\left(\rho_{XT}^2\right)$, where the true score is the hypothetical average of the observed scores that would be obtained if the measurement were repeated over an infinite number of similar conditions. For example, *parallel forms reliability* is an estimate of the reliability across parallel forms of the test, estimated by the correlation of two particular parallel forms. Test–retest reliability is an estimate of the reliability across testing occasions, estimated by the correlation between scores obtained on two occasions. Coefficient α

(equivalent to KR-20 for dichotomous items) is an estimate of the reliability across different random sets of items, estimated based on the relationships among items in one test form.

In CTT, the standard error of measurement, or standard error of the estimated score, σ_e, is then based on the definition that observed score variance = true score variance plus error variance $(\sigma_X^2 = \sigma_T^2 + \sigma_e^2$, so $\sigma_e = \sigma_X \sqrt{(1 - \rho_{XT}^2)})$. When this definition of standard error is used, a single estimate of the standard error is calculated regardless of the value of the observed score, X. The estimate is calculated by substituting the standard deviation of the scores in the sample for σ_X and some estimate of reliability, perhaps coefficient α, for ρ_{XT}^2. Another common definition of the standard error of measurement is based on the binomial theorem: $\sigma_e = \sqrt{\frac{X(n-X)}{n-1}}$, where X is the number-correct score and n is the number of items. With this definition, extreme scores (scores that are close to 0 or the maximum value) have smaller standard errors than middle scores. This definition does not require an estimate of reliability to calculate the standard error. Instead, the standard error is calculated first and then can be used to form a reliability-like coefficient.[1]

In IRT, the information function is used to calculate the standard error of measurement and the reliability. The test information is a function of proficiency (or whatever trait or skill is measured) and the items on the test. Thus, test information varies with the proficiency level, as shown in Figure 1.1. The standard error of measurement is the inverse of the square root of information, so that the greater the information, the smaller the standard error and the greater the reliability. An advantage of IRT is that the information function can also be defined at the item level, and the item information functions sum to the test information function. This is useful because items from different test forms can be assembled in different configurations, and the test information can be calculated for each new test form before the test is administered. In CTT, the new test forms would need to be

---

[1] For readers familiar with generalizability theory, the mean of this error variance is equivalent to the absolute error variance (Feldt & Brennan, 1989, p. 131), so the resulting reliability coefficient is the ϕ-coefficient, not the G-coefficient.

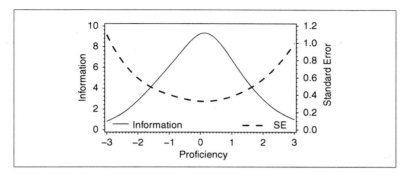

Figure 1.1. Relationship between test information and standard error of the proficiency estimate. In locations where there is more information, the standard error is lower.

administered to new samples to estimate the reliability, unless a very careful sampling design were used such that all pairwise item correlations could be estimated. Also, in IRT, subsets of items can be removed from a test form and the corresponding item information functions can be subtracted to quickly calculate the new test information. In CTT, reestimating the reliability after removing subsets of items would require more complicated calculations than simple subtraction. Finally, if a reliability estimate of the IRT scores is desired for a sample or population of examinees, it can be estimated based on the item parameters and the distribution of the trait in that group of examinees. (Calculations are detailed in Chapter 4.)

Parameter Invariance

Another advantage of IRT is population invariance of the item parameters. This means that the item parameters should be the same in different populations of examinees. In CTT, the item difficulty P (or item mean score) depends entirely on the proficiency or trait level of the population of examinees. If another examinee population with higher trait levels took the test, the item difficulties would be higher (remember, higher difficulty means easier items in CTT). In IRT, the item difficulty, b, is the same (invariant) across samples, up to a linear transformation. A *linear transformation* means that the b's from one population of examinees are multiplied/divided by a constant and another constant is added or subtracted, to put them on the same metric as the b's from another population of examinees. A linear transformation cannot be used to put the CTT item difficulties on the same metric. This is easiest to see by comparing a middle difficulty item and a very easy item. The easy item might have a P of .98 in the less-able population and .99 in the more-able population: a small difference because of the limits of the CTT metric. But the middle difficulty item might have a P of .50 in the less-able population and .80 in the more-able population. The differences are not constant. A third item would be needed to prove that the relationship is not linear, but the general idea is evident with these two items. Item discriminations, a's, in IRT are also invariant across populations after a linear transformation. Classical test theory point-biserial item-total correlations depend on the item difficulty in the examinee population, as well as on the underlying correlation. An item will have a lower point-biserial item in the population in which its difficulty is most extreme.

However, the difference between IRT and CTT with regards to population invariance should not be overstated. If the items are not too extreme or the populations are not too different, CTT indices should show a mostly linear relationship across populations. Empirically, Fan (1998) found that linear correlations between CTT item estimates from different samples were generally comparable to the correlations between IRT item estimates from different samples. Additionally, if the CTT true scores underlying the observed responses can reasonably be assumed to be normally distributed, and if there is minimal correct guessing, a nonlinear transformation can be used to put the P's from two different populations on the same metric (for example, educational testing service (ETS) used the Δ-scale before IRT was in common use).

Under the same assumption of normality and no correct guessing, the point-biserial correlations can be transformed to biserial correlations, which are theoretically not sensitive to the average ability in the population, although like any correlation they depend on the variance of ability. The biserial correlation is an estimate of what the item-total correlation would be if the item were measured on a continuous scale, rather than on a dichotomous scale. In measurement, the item responses are conceptualized as caused by underlying continuous traits, so the biserial correlation is reasonable conceptually if the trait can be assumed to be normally distributed. (As a counter example, an instrument designed to measure clinical levels of a trait would be unlikely to yield normally distributed scores in a nonclinical population.) These nonlinear transformations require very large samples for accurate estimation, but IRT models require large samples for accurate estimation, too. The IRT models, however, do not require the assumptions of normality or no-guessing required for the most commonly used formulas for calculating the biserial correlation.

A final note on invariance: the invariance only strictly applies to the parameters in the populations, not to the sample estimates of the parameters. Due to estimation error, the estimates from two samples of the populations (or two samples of the same population) will not be identical even after the appropriate transformation. After the best transformation is estimated and applied to the item parameter estimates, the two sets of estimates should be similar but they will not be identical.

In the next two sections, some of the most common IRT models are described. As noted earlier, IRT can be used with both dichotomous (two-category) and polytomous (more than two category) items, so a section is devoted to each type. All of the models show how the response probability is a function of the trait measured by the instrument, such as a proficiency or disposition. In this book, the trait is symbolized by θ, using typical IRT notation. This symbol is the Greek letter theta, and it will be useful not only when equations are necessary. but also in the text to avoid the repetition of *proficiency or ability or trait or attitude or disposition*. The reader can substitute whatever term is appropriate.

Models for Dichotomous Items

Because there are only two categories, dichotomous models show the probability of a score of 1; the probability of a score of 0 is 1 minus the probability of a score of 1. On academic tests, correct responses are scored *1*. On attitudinal or psychological tests, the category that indicates higher levels of the construct is scored *1*. For example, on a depression scale, if *agree* indicates more depression, then *agree* would be scored *1*. Other items on the same scale might be written to be reverse-scored: on these items, *disagree* might indicate higher levels of depression, so *disagree* would be scored *1*. To keep the text readable, the simple phrase *probability of correct response* will often be used; the reader can substitute a more appropriate phrase if *correct response* is inapplicable to a particular construct.

The probability of a correct response is expressed as a function of θ. When the probability is calculated for a specific value of θ, it can be interpreted as the probability of a correct response for an examinee randomly selected from a group of examinees with that value of θ. The typical models used for dichotomous items are the three-parameter logistic (3PL), 2PL, and 1PL. These models are named by the number of item parameters used in the function that models the relationship between θ and the item response (0/1).

An example of an item characteristic curve (ICC, also known as the item response function [IRF]) is shown in Figure 1.2. The empirical ICC is shown with a dashed line. This empirical curve is based on a sample of 2,726 examinees. Examinees were grouped into 20 intervals based on θ (x-axis), and the proportion in each group who answered the item correctly was plotted on the y-axis (vertical axis). This proportion is the observed or empirical probability of correct response, given θ ("given θ" is a statistical term that means "for a particular value of θ." Sometimes this is expressed as "conditional on θ"). The ICC based on the 3PL model is shown with a solid line. The model provides a smooth curve because it is a simple function using only three item parameters: discrimination, difficulty, and lower asymptote. These

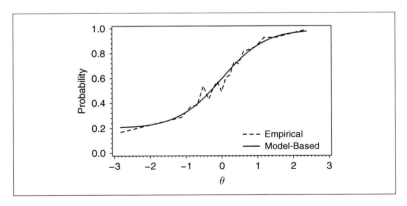

Figure 1.2. Model-based and empirical ICCs. The empirical ICC is based on the observed proportion—correct for sets of examinees grouped by proficiency level.

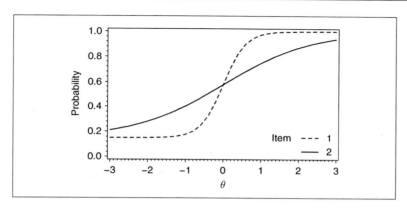

Figure 1.3. Items with different *a*-parameters. Item 1 is more discriminating.

parameters are typically labeled *a*, *b*, and *c*. The object of parametric IRT is to describe the data using just these parameters. As can be seen in Figure 1.2, the data can often be approximated well with a smooth curve. The remaining example figures will illustrate only this model-based smooth curve.

The discrimination parameter, or slope[2], *a*, tells how steeply the probability of correct response changes at the steepest point on the curve. Figure 1.3 shows two items with different *a* parameters; item 1 has a higher discrimination than item 2. Thus, item 1 can better differentiate (discriminate) between an examinee with a moderately high θ and a moderately low θ. Using CTT, the item-total point-biserial correlation would also be higher for item 1 than for item 2, assuming that both items have similar proportion-correct in the sample[3] as they do in this example.

The difficulty parameter, *b*, tells how difficult the item is (for attitudinal or psychological scales, difficulty indicates the amount of the trait that is needed to be more likely to choose the response scored *1* than the response scored *0*). Its value equals the θ value where the slope of the function is steepest. About 50% (or a little more, depending on the value of *c*) of examinees with θ = *b* would

---

[2] The slope at θ = *b* actually equals the *a*-parameter times a constant, but the *a*-parameter is often referred to simply as the slope.

[3] Point-biserial correlations are sensitive to the item difficulty, whereas IRT discrimination indices are not.

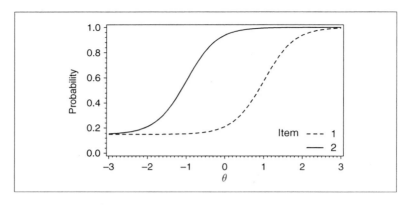

Figure 1.4. Items with different *b*-parameters. Item 1 is more difficult.

score *1*. Figure 1.4 shows two items with different *b* parameters. Item 1 is more difficult than item 2; for any given value of θ, the probability of getting item 1 right is lower than the probability of getting item 2 right. Difficult items have higher values of *b*; recall that this is the opposite of CTT, in which difficult items have lower difficulty indices, *P*. *P* and *b* are generally highly (but negatively) correlated.

The lower asymptote parameter, *c*, provides the probability that an examinee with a very low level of θ will answer the item correctly. Figure 1.5 shows two items with different *c* parameters. The lower asymptote is lower for item 1 than for item 2. The term *lower* or *left*

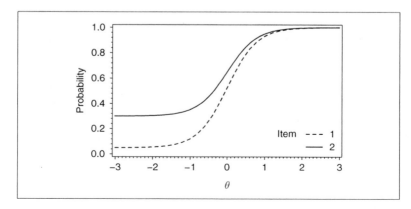

Figure 1.5. Items with different *c*-parameters. Item 2 has a higher *c*-parameter.

asymptote is used to describe the value that the function approaches as θ approaches negative infinity. The term *upper asymptote* is used to describe the value that the function approaches as θ approaches positive infinity. In the models described in this book, the upper asymptote is 1 and will not be discussed further. The *c*-parameter is sometimes called a *guessing* parameter because examinees with very low θ would be expected to get the item correct only by guessing. Lord (1974) stated that in well-developed standardized tests, the *c*-parameter tends to be somewhat lower than chance because good distractors draw low-ability examinees away from the correct answer. However, if an item contains poor distractors that even a low-ability examinee can eliminate as possibilities, the *c*-parameter may be higher than chance.

The mathematical form of the 3PL model is:

$$P(\theta) = c_i + (1 - c_i)\frac{e^{1.7a_i(\theta - b_i)}}{1 + e^{1.7a_i(\theta - b_i)}} \qquad (1)$$

where $P(\theta)$ indicates the probability of correct response given θ and the item parameters (more fully expressed as $P(x = 1 | \theta, a, b, c)$). The subscript *i* indicates the item, *i*. Sometimes the subscript *j* is added to θ to indicate the examinee:

$$P(\theta_j) = c_i + (1 - c_i)\frac{e^{1.7a_i(\theta_j - b_i)}}{1 + e^{1.7a_i(\theta_j - b_i)}}. \qquad (2)$$

Often either or both of these subscripts are implicit, rather than explicitly shown.

The *e* in the function is a mathematical constant, the exponential function. Its value is approximately 2.718. Its counterpart is the natural log function; the natural log of $e = 1$.[4] The 1.7 is a scaling parameter; it is not necessary, but omitting it would change the scale of the *a*-parameter. It is often included for historical reasons that will be explained in the discussion of the 2PL model.

---

[4] In mathematics, the symbol *ln* is often used for the natural log function. In statistics and measurement, the symbol *log* is often used for the natural log function. This can be confusing for those used to the mathematical convention of using *log* for the base-10 log function.

The 2PL and 1PL IRT models are special cases, or *constrained* versions, of the 3PL model. To constrain a model means to fix the value of one or more of the parameters. For the 2PL model, the lower-asymptote's value is fixed to zero. Thus, the model becomes:

$$P(\theta) = \frac{e^{1.7a_i(\theta - b_i)}}{1 + e^{1.7a_i(\theta - b_i)}} . \tag{3}$$

In Figure 1.6, items 1 and 2 are 2PL items. They have different *a* and *b* parameters, but both functions approach a lower-asymptote of zero. The 2PL model approximates a cumulative normal distribution, called a *normal ogive*. Use of the normal ogive function to model item responses predates use of logistic functions. The disadvantage of normal ogives is that they require mathematical integration—the probability of a correct response is calculated by finding the area under the curve below the value $a(\theta - b)$. Logistic functions are thus simply easier to work with. The 1.7 in Equations 1 through 3 puts the logistic parameters into the same metric as the normal ogive model's parameters. Without the 1.7, the *a* parameters would be larger (by a factor of 1.7). The 1.7 merely makes the *a* parameters more interpretable to those used to the normal ogive metric. The use of this constant is typical but not universal.

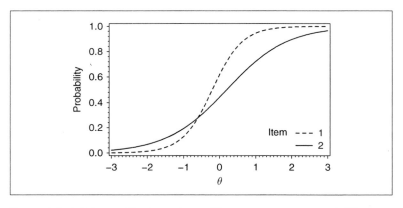

Figure 1.6. 2PL items. The items have different *a*-parameters and different *b*-parameters.

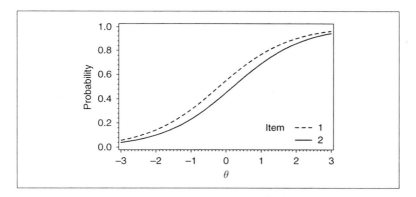

Figure 1.7. 1PL items. The items share the same *a*-parameter but have different *b*-parameters.

For the 1PL model, the value of c is fixed to zero, and a is fixed to the same value across items. Thus, the model becomes:

$$P(\theta)=\frac{e^{1.7a\,(\theta-b_i\,)}}{1+e^{1.7a\,(\theta-b_i\,)}}.\qquad(4)$$

Notice that there is no subscript on the a-parameter, because it is the same for all items. In Figure 1.7, items 1 and 2 have the same difficulties as the items in Figure 1.6, but instead of different a parameters, they have the same a-parameter. Notice that the function representing the probability of correct response for item 1 never crosses the function for the probability of correct response for item 2, although they approach each other because they have the same upper and lower asymptotes (1 and 0, respectively).

The Rasch model (Rasch, 1960/1980) is mathematically equivalent to the 1PL IRT model, but it was developed separately and was *not* specified as a special case of the 2PL model; most users of Rasch models prefer not to use the label IRT. The Rasch model was originally specified in terms of odds [probability/(1 – probability)] or log-odds (the natural log of the odds, also called *logits*), but it is now often specified in terms of probability. When specified this way, the model is the same as Equation 4, except that generally the 1.7 is omitted and the a-parameter is dropped from the model, effectively fixing it to 1. The only consequence of this is to change the size of the measurement units. The notational system is also typically different, using δ in place of b and β in place of θ.

Obviously, this has no effect on the mathematical function, but readers should be aware of the change in symbols. A typical way of specifying the Rasch model thus would be:

$$P(\beta) = \frac{e^{(\beta - \delta_i)}}{1 + e^{(\beta - \delta_i)}}, \text{ or} \tag{5}$$

$$\ln\left(\frac{P(\beta)}{1 - P(\beta)}\right) = \beta - \delta_i \tag{6}$$

Parallel to Equation 1, $P(\beta)$ is the probability of correct response given β and δ, and would be more fully expressed as $P(x = 1|\beta, \delta)$. For consistency with the rest of this book, the symbol θ is used in the following discussion, but this symbol likely would *not* be used in an article or book focused on the Rasch model.

The Rasch model, and equivalently the 1PL model, has some desirable mathematical properties that cannot be obtained with the 2PL and 3PL models. The number-correct (raw or observed) score is a sufficient statistic for θ (symbolized β in the Rasch model) (Schumacker, 2004; Wright, 1997; Wright & Stone, 1979, p. 20). This means that all examinees with the same number-correct score will have the same estimated θ (assuming they all were given the same test items), while in the 2PL and 3PL models, two examinees with the same total number of items correct but with different patterns of items correct will have somewhat different estimates of θ[5]. Similarly, the proportion correct (P in CTT) is a sufficient statistic for the item difficulty. This means that if the number of examinees responding correctly is the same for two items, the items will have the same Rasch difficulty estimate, regardless of which examinees responded correctly. Note that sufficiency does *not* imply a linear relationship. If it did, there would be no advantages to using the 1PL and Rasch models instead of number-correct scores. But sufficiency greatly simplifies the process of estimating the item and trait parameters. It also has practical advantages. For a given test form (fixed set of items), there is a

---

[5] Essentially, more discriminating items are weighted more highly in 2PL and 3PL estimates of θ, and items which are relatively difficult for an examinee (low value for $\theta - b$) are weighted less in the 3PL model because the c-parameter has a bigger influence on the probability in this range.

one-to-one correspondence between the number-correct score and θ. Test users, such as teachers, can be given a simple chart that shows the estimated θ for each number-correct score. Also, if number-correct scores are provided along with θ-based standardized scores on a large-scale test, there is no possibility that examinees (or parents of examinees) will compare scores and complain because two examinees with the same number-correct score obtained different standardized scores.

Again, even though the number-correct score is a sufficient statistic for θ, θ is *not* a linear transformation of the number-correct score. As Wright and Stone (1979) or Wright (1997) explained, the units on the number-correct score metric are not necessarily at equal intervals relative to the units on the θ scale (most typically, the number-correct units are stretched out at the extremes and squeezed together in the middle). An example of a relationship between these metrics for one test is shown in Figure 1.8. Notice how, relative to the θ units, the number-correct units are spaced more widely at the upper end of the metric. Clearly, if the θ scale is interval-level, the number-correct scale is only ordinal level. In terms of the log-odds (logits), the Rasch and 1PL metrics are interval-level. If two examinees differ by 1 logit, the difference in their log-odds of getting an item correct is 1, regardless of the item difficulty or the location of the examinees on the metric. But on the number-correct metric, the log-odds (logit) difference between an examinee with a score of 10 and an examinee with a score of 11 is not equal to the log-odds difference between an examinee with a score of 18 and an examinee with a score of 19.

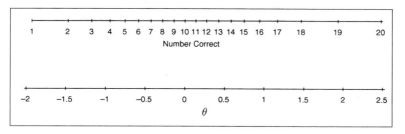

Figure 1.8. Relationship between θ and number-correct (observed) score. Relative to the θ metric, the number-correct scores are not spaced at equal intervals.

Another mathematical property of the Rasch (and 1PL) model is that the ICCs from two different items will never cross. When the probabilities are transformed to log-odds (logits), this means that the difference in log-odds is constant across the θ scale, as explained earlier. Figure 1.9 shows this property for the Rasch model, and Figure 1.10 shows that this property does not hold for the 2PL model. Figure 1.10 (or the earlier Fig. 1.6) shows what may be a considered a problem with the 2PL model (Wilson, 2004, 2005; Wright, 1997): Item 1 is more difficult for low-ability examinees, but item 2 is more difficult for high-ability examinees. Which item is more difficult? The situation is even more

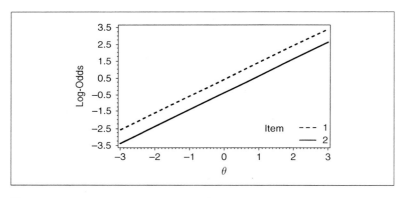

Figure 1.9. Log-odds for Rasch items. The log-odds functions are parallel.

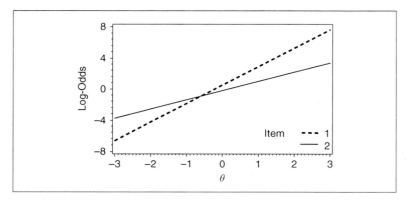

Figure 1.10. Log-odds for 2PL items. The log-odds functions are not parallel because the items have different *a*-parameters.

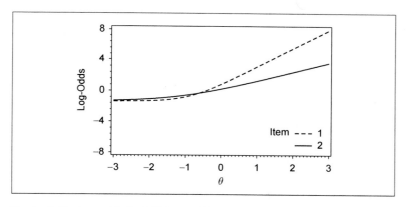

Figure 1.11. Log-odds for 3PL items. The log-odds functions are particularly close at the low end of the θ continuum due to the lower asymptote.

complicated with the 3PL model, in which the relationship between log-odds and θ is nonlinear (Fig. 1.11). This issue could also be considered in terms of differences between examinees. Again examining Figure 1.10, if two examinees differ in θ by x units, their difference in log-odds of correct response will be greater on item 1 than item 2. If the data followed the Rasch or 1PL model, the difference between these examinees would be constant in log-odds units. Rasch proponents consider this issue a serious shortcoming of the 2PL and 3PL models.

Thissen and Orlando (2001) discussed the philosophical differences between Rasch modeling and IRT from the point of view of IRT proponents. They explained that their objective is to find the model that fits the data. They advised "Items are assumed to measure as they *do*, not as they should" (p. 90). They contrasted this with followers of the Rasch model, who begin with properties central to the Rasch view of measurement, design items to fit these properties, and discard those that are found empirically not to fit the desired model. Thissen and Orlando noted that both sides understand the approach of the other; where they differ "is on the relative evaluation of these two approaches" (p. 91).

Probabilities versus Log-odds

Logistic models, except for the 3PL, can easily be written in terms of log-odds instead of probabilities. The odds of correct response $= P(\theta)/(1 - P(\theta))$. The log-odds is the natural log of the odds. For example, the 2PL can be written as:

$$\ln\left(\frac{P(\theta)}{1 - P(\theta)}\right) = 1.7a_i(\theta - b_i). \tag{7}$$

The equation looks similar to a logistic-regression equation, except that in logistic regression the predictor or independent variable is an observable quantity, such as number-correct score, rather than a latent variable that must be estimated. When the log-odds are graphed, they are a linear (straight-line) function of θ for the 1PL and 2PL models, as shown earlier in Figures 1.9 and 1.10. The c-parameter introduces nonlinearity in the log-odds for the 3PL model, as shown in Figure 1.11.

In the 1PL, the log-odds are parallel for all items. The ICCs for 1PL items are often said to be parallel, even though it is clear from Figure 1.7 that the curves approach the same upper and lower asymptotes, and thus come closer together at these points. What we mean when we say the 1PL ICCs are parallel is that the log-odds are parallel. As noted above, Rasch formulated his model in terms of odds and log-odds (Rasch, 1960/1980), although it can be equivalently specified in terms of probabilities.

Interpreting Parameter Values for Dichotomous Items

The metric of the parameters is somewhat arbitrary. The metric is indeterminate until we fix the center (zero-point) of the scale and the unit size. Most frequently, in a reference population (perhaps represented by the norming sample) the estimated mean of θ is set to 0 and the estimated standard deviation of θ is set to 1. θ can then be interpreted similarly to a z-score. Because θ is not a linear function of the number-correct (raw or observed) score, θ will not be exactly the same as the z-score on the number-correct metric, but the interpretation is similar. When an examinee is 1 standard deviation above the mean in the reference population, the examinee's $\theta = 1$. There is no assumption that the scores are normally distributed, so the θ does not necessarily translate to a percentile score in the normal distribution. Values for θ theoretically range from $-\infty$ to $+\infty$; most examinees will have values between -3 and 3.

The item difficulty, or b-parameter, is on the same metric as θ. When $b = \theta$, the probability of correct response is 50% for the 1PL and 2PL models (somewhat higher for the 3PL model). The items in Figure 1.6 were 2PL items, and the items in Figure 1.7 were 1PL items, but they had the same difficulty. Item 1's $b = -0.2$, so 50% of examinees with $\theta = -0.2$ would answer item 1 correctly. Item 2's $b = 0.2$, so 50% of examinees with $\theta = 0.2$ would answer item 2 correctly. Notice that the ICC is steepest at b. Like θ, b's have a theoretical range from $-\infty$ to $+\infty$ but are generally between -2 and 2 so as to not be too easy or too hard for the intended test population.

The metric for the item discrimination, slope, or a-parameter, is less intuitive and takes experience to get used to. The theoretical range is again from $-\infty$ to $+\infty$, but the practical range is from 0 to perhaps 2 or 3. Items with negative discrimination may be screened out by some estimation programs, and they should certainly be removed by the test developers. A negative discrimination, like a negative discrimination in CTT, would mean that examinees with higher θs were less likely to answer the item correctly. Such items should be checked for errors in the scoring key, and unless the item is keyed incorrectly it should be revised or dropped from the test. Similarly, discriminations less than 0.4 or so are unlikely on an operational test because they should have been screened out during the test development process. Looking back at Figure 1.6, item 1 has a discrimination of 1.4 and item 2 has a discrimination of 0.7.

The lower asymptote, or c-parameter, is the probability of correct response for examinees with infinitely low θ. It could theoretically range from 0 to 1, but would more realistically range from 0 to .3 or so. As noted, it might be a little below or above the probability of random guessing, depending on the quality of the distractors. Looking back at Figure 1.5, the lower asymptote for item 1 is .05 and the lower asymptote for item 2 is .30.

The Test Characteristic Curve

The ICCs can be summed to form the test characteristic curve (TCC) (also known as the *test characteristic function*, TCF). Each ICC ranges from the lower asymptote to 1, so the TCC will range from the sum of the lower asymptotes (0 for 1PL or 2PL models) to the number of items. The TCC thus shows the expected

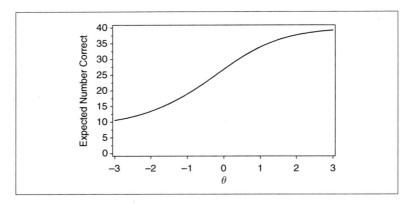

Figure 1.12. Test characteristic curve. The vertical axis indicates the expected number-correct test score as a function of θ.

number-correct score as a function of θ; *expected* is used here in the mathematical sense of expected value or mean conditional on θ. An example is shown in Figure 1.12. There were 40 items on the test. Examinees with $\theta = -1$, for example, would be predicted to have a number-correct score of approximately 19. Because most of the items had lower asymptotes of .2 to .3, even those with $\theta = -3$ would be predicted to have scores of approximately 10.

Models for Polytomous Items

Items that have more than two categories are labeled *polytomous*, or *polychotomous*, items. Weiss (1983) provided a short essay explaining why *polytomous* is more correct given the etymology of the term, but both terms should be used when conducting a literature search. Several models have been proposed and used for polytomous items. This book focuses on two of these models (and their variants): Samejima's (1969) Graded Response (GR) model and Muraki's (1992) Generalized Partial Credit (GPC) model, a generalization of Master's (1982) Partial Credit (PC) model. These models are for items in which the categories are ordered; they cannot be used to determine the empirical ordering of the categories post hoc. They are appropriate for items or products (presentations, portfolios, essays, etc.) scored using a scoring rubric. They are also appropriate for Likert-type items, items with an

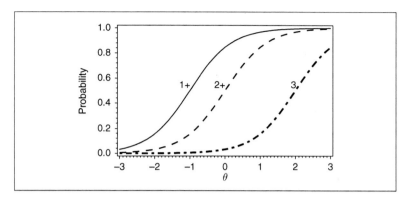

Figure 1.13. GR model for a 4-category item (scored 0–3), probability of each category/score or higher.

ordered response scale such as: *strongly disagree, disagree, neutral, agree, strongly agree.*

In these models, a function analogous to an ICC can be plotted for each category. Unfortunately, the term used to label these curves is not universal, so the reader must infer from the context which function is plotted.

In the graded response model, the probability of scoring in or selecting each category *or higher* is modeled. An example is shown in Figure 1.13. The categories depicted are scored 0–3 (they could be labeled 1–4 instead). The probability of scoring 0 or higher is of course 1, so only categories 1 through 3 are shown. The functions are parallel; otherwise, the probability of scoring 1 or higher would at some point be lower than the probability of scoring 2 or higher.[6]

From these functions, the probability of scoring/selecting category *x* can be calculated from the probability of scoring *x or higher.* These probabilities are illustrated in Figure 1.14. Note that this figure depicts all four categories, including the score of 0. Samejima called these functions *operating characteristics.* Likewise, de Ayala (1993) labeled the curves in Figure 1.14 operating characteristic curves (OCC) and used the term *category characteristic curves* (CCC) for the curves in Figure 1.13. Embretson and Reise (2000, Chapter 5)

---

[6] Samejima (1969, p. 19) proposed another version of the model that allowed this, but it is used infrequently if ever, because of this logical contradiction.

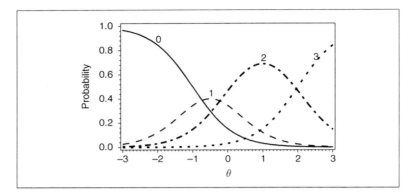

Figure 1.14. GR model for a 4-category item, probability of each category/ score. These probabilities were calculated by subtracting adjacent probabilities in Figure 1.13.

used nearly opposite labels: operating characteristic curves (OCC) for Figure 1.13 and category response curves (CRC) for Figure 1.14. Several other terms have been used for these types of functions in various polytomous models. Sijtsma and Meijer (2007) used the designations category response function (CRF) for the probability of scoring x and item step response function (ISRF) for the probability of scoring x *or higher*. Wilson (2005, Chapter 5) also used the term category response function (CRF) but applied the term cumulative category response function (CCRF) for the probability of scoring x *or higher*. Other labels include item category response function (ICRF; Muraki, 1992) and option response function (ORF; de Ayala & Sava-Bolesta, 1999) for the probability of scoring x, or boundary response function (BRF; Oshima & Morris, 2008) for the probability of scoring x *or higher*. Thus, a research report should define whatever terms are chosen.

The mathematical function for the GR model looks very much like the function for the 2PL. The only difference is that there are multiple b-parameters, one for each category except the first.

$$P_{ik}^*(\theta) = \frac{e^{1.7a_i(\theta - b_{ik})}}{1 + e^{1.7a_i(\theta - b_{ik})}}, \tag{8}$$

where $P_{ik}^*(\theta)$ is the probability of scoring in or above category k of item i (given θ and the item parameters), a_i as before is the item slope, and b_{ik} is the category boundary or threshold for category k of item i. For example, in Figure 1.13, $b_{i1} = -1.0$, which means that 50% of examinees with $\theta = -1.0$ have scores of 1 or higher. The subscript i for item i is sometimes dropped when it is clear from the context. An * or $+$ is typically added to P to indicate it is the probability of scoring/selecting the category or higher, not the probability of scoring/selecting the category.

In the GR model, the b-parameters are typically called *thresholds*, because they indicate the threshold at which examinees have equal probabilities of scoring/choosing a category lower than k versus k or higher. The thresholds are not fixed at equal intervals within an item; the model takes into account that observed scores are not necessarily interval-level. In a special case of the GR model, the spacing of the categories can be fixed *across* (not within) items. In this special case, for different items, the centering of the categories is shifted based on the item difficulty, but the spacing of the thresholds is constant across items. Thus, the model requires a smaller number of item parameters. This is called the *modified GR model* (Embretson & Reise, 2000) or the rating scale version of the GR model (Muraki, 1990). It might be appropriate if the respondents or raters use the scale in the same way across all items.

The a-parameter can be interpreted similarly to the a-parameter for dichotomous items. In another special case of the GR model, the a-parameter can be fixed constant across all items. Some authors prefer not to use the label *discrimination* for the a-parameter for polytomous items (Embretson & Reise, 2000, p. 102). In polytomous items, the degree to which the item discriminates among examinees with different θs is a function of both the a-parameter and the relative locations of the b-parameters. Thus, *slope*, or simply a-parameter, may be a less controversial label. However, the label *discrimination* is in common use as well.

In the GPC model, the probability of scoring in or selecting each category is modeled directly (instead of the category or higher). An example is shown in Figure 1.15, which looks quite similar in general form to Figure 1.14. de Ayala (1993) labeled these curves operating characteristic curves (OCC) and Embretson and Reise (2000, Chapter 5) labeled them category response curves (CRC). As noted earlier for the GR model, many different terms may be applied, and there is not yet one term in predominant usage. The

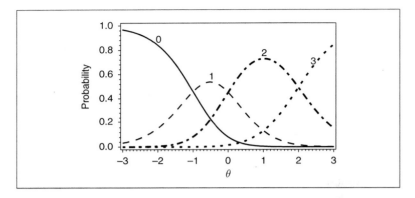

Figure 1.15. GPC model for a 4-category item, probability of each category/score.

categories depicted are again labeled 0–3 but arbitrarily could have been labeled 1–4.

The mathematical function for the GPC model is a bit more complicated than the GR function:

$$P_{ik}(\theta) = \frac{e^{\sum_{x=0}^{k} 1.7a_i(\theta - b_{ix})}}{\sum_{j=0}^{m_i} e^{\sum_{x=0}^{j} 1.7a_i(\theta - b_{ix})}}, \tag{9}$$

Like the GR model, there is one b-parameter for each category except the first; the number of categories for item i is m_i. As there is no b_{i0}, $\theta - b_{i0}$ is defined as 0, so the numerator for the lowest category $= e^0 = 1$. These category parameters are often called item *step difficulties*. The step difficulties indicate the point at which the probabilities for adjacent categories are equally likely. For example, in Figure 1.15, $b_{i1} = -1.0$, which means scores 0 and 1 are equally likely for examinees at $\theta = -1.0$. In other words, the curves intersect at this point. The a-parameter, as in the GR model, indicates how rapidly the response probabilities change as θ changes.

When there are only two categories, both the GR and GPC models are equivalent to the 2PL model. With three or more categories, however, the parameters in these two models are not comparable. A category threshold in the GR model is the location at which the probability of scoring/choosing that category or higher is 50%. A category step difficulty in the GPC model is the location at which the probabilities of two adjacent categories are equal. To see why these are not equivalent, look back at Figures 1.13 and 1.14. These curves were based on the GR model, with the values in Figure 1.14 obtained by subtracting the probability of category $k - 1$ or higher from the probability of category k or higher in Figure 1.13. Notice that the 50% points in Figure 1.13 do not match the intersection points in Figure 1.14. Further, compare the GR model in Figure 1.14 to the GPC model in Figure 1.15. The item parameter values are the same in both models, but the curves look quite different. Different parameters are needed to make the curves from the two models more similar.

To minimize the difference between the models, the item parameters in the GPC model were changed, and the GPC model with these new parameters is displayed in Figure 1.16. These GPC curves in Figure 1.16 are fairly close to the GR curves in Figure 1.14. However, in Figure 1.14 $a_i = 1$, $b_{i1} = -1$, $b_{i2} = 0$, $b_{i3} = 2$ but in Figure 1.16 $a_i = 0.70$, $b_{i1} = -0.76$, $b_{i2} = -0.35$, $b_{i3} = 2.58$. The difference between the curves in the two models was minimized most at the center of the graph because that is where most of the examinees would be; the curves have greater differences at either end, but this would have little practical effect because few examinees are located at the extremes. Although Figure 1.16 does not match Figure 1.14 perfectly, it is much closer than Figure 1.15 was.

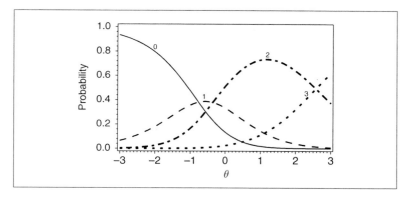

Figure 1.16. GPC model that best matches GR data depicted in Figures 1.13 and 1.14.

The point of this display is to show that, while the GR and GPC models can both approximate the same curves, the parameters used to do so may be quite different. Item parameters should *not* be compared across these families of models.

The GPC is called the *generalized* partial credit model because Muraki (1992) developed it as a generalized version of the partial credit (PC) model. Masters (1982) developed the PC model as an extension of the Rasch model. In the PC model, the a-parameter is constant across items (or fixed to equal 1, so that it drops out of the model), just as the a-parameter is constant across items in the 1PL model (or fixed to equal 1 in the Rasch model). In the generalized model, the a-parameters may vary across items.

The rating scale (RS) model (Andrich, 1978) is a related model in this family of models. It is equivalent to a restricted version of the PC model, where the distances between adjacent step difficulties are the same across all items (as in the modified GR model described above). Again, each item has a location parameter to indicate how much the mean of the set of step difficulties is offset from zero, but a single set of step difficulties is used for all items, decreasing the total number of item parameters needed. Like the PC model, the a-parameter does not vary across items.

The OCCs (CCCs, ORFs, whatever terminology is preferred) can be summed across categories to display the ICC (IRF); for the GR model, the $P^*(\theta)$ is converted to $P(\theta)$ before summing. An example is shown in Figure 1.17, based on the option curves in

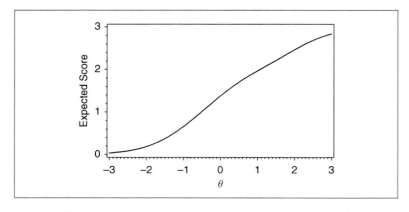

Figure 1.17. Item response function for GR item. The vertical axis indicates the expected number-correct item score as a function of θ.

Figure 1.14. The y-axis is now scaled from 0–3 instead of 0–1, and labeled *Expected Score* instead of *Probability*. The label *expected* is used to indicate the mathematical expectation, or mean. For dichotomous items, the mean score is the same as the probability of scoring 1, so it is conventional to use the term *probability* instead of *expected score*. The ICCs of all of the test items, dichotomous or polytomous, can be summed together to form the test characteristic curve (TCC) or test response function (TRF), as was illustrated for dichotomous items. The TCC is scaled from 0 to the maximum score on the test. Or, if the first category in each item was scored 1 instead of 0, the TCC is scaled from the number of items to the maximum score on the instrument.

Choosing a Model

Among the dichotomous models, the 3PL model is the most common choice for multiple-choice items because it seems reasonable to assume that low-ability examinees have some non-zero probability of choosing the correct answer. The 2PL model might be more appropriate for dichotomous attitudinal items. It might also be useful for multiple choice items with very effective distractors, where low-ability examinees would tend to think a particular distractor was right rather than to guess randomly. This might occur for domains in which there are particular errors or misconceptions that low-ability examinees consistently make. Such distractors would likely require the expertise of both content specialists and cognitive psychologists, but would be very useful if they could be written effectively. The 1PL model has desirable mathematical properties, as discussed earlier. The Rasch model or 1PL is often chosen to obtain these properties. According to this philosophy, items that do not fit the model are not considered useful for measurement. Those who do not strictly hold the Rasch philosophy, however, sometimes use the 1PL model for simplicity, or because they do not have enough data to estimate a more complex model well. Using a simple model that is estimated more accurately can sometimes produce better results than using a complex model that is estimated poorly, even if the complex model fits the data better (Barnes & Wise, 1991; Lord, 1980). Similar considerations apply when choosing between a polytomous model that allows the a-parameter to vary across items (GPC or GR models) or one that constrains the a-parameter to be equal for all items (PC or GR constrained to have equal a's).

The fit of the model should also be considered. This will be discussed in much greater detail in Chapter 3 (in this volume). For now, it is important to understand that the model that appears to fit best in a sample is not necessarily the best-fitting model in the population, so the conceptual considerations described here should be considered along with empirical fit.

Chapter Summary

To recap, this chapter has compared IRT and CTT in terms of item parameters, conceptualization of reliability and standard error of measurement, and population invariance. The 3PL, 2PL, and 1PL dichotomous models were introduced, along with the GR and GPC polytomous models. In Chapter 2, the types of questions for which IRT is useful are described, along with the data requirements needed to apply IRT appropriately.

REQUIREMENTS

2

SOME OF THE QUESTIONS that item response theory (IRT) can be used to address include:

- What is the spread of item difficulties (and category difficulties, for polytomous items)?
- How discriminating is each item?
- What is the distribution of abilities/traits in this group of examinees/respondents? How does the ability distribution compare to the item difficulty distribution?
- How much information does the test provide over the ability/trait range?
- How does each item contribute to the test information?
- For a given population or sample distribution, how reliable are the ability/trait estimates?

These questions, although vitally important to the test developer and test users, are not the sort of research questions commonly addressed in journal articles. Rather, they are questions covered in a test/item analysis report or technical documentation for a testing program. They deal with a specific assessment instrument rather than generalizable research problems. Item response theory research questions for psychometric journals include more advanced topics such as the development or comparison of estimation methods, procedures for checking assumptions and fit, new models, or equating techniques. These questions are outside the scope of this book. Here, I focus on the application of IRT, not methodological research in IRT. Further, the focus is on test development and scoring. Details on more advanced applications, such as equating/ linking, differential item functioning, and adaptive testing, will be left to other volumes in the series. These applications show the power of IRT, but before exploring these advanced applications, one must first understand the basics of IRT.

Data Sample Design

In Chapter 1, the property of invariance was introduced. In classical test theory (CTT), the item parameters depend on the population, so the data should be randomly sampled from the population to obtain accurate estimates. In IRT, because of the invariance property, the sample *theoretically* does not need to be a random sample from the population of interest. A nonrandom sample could be used, and the estimated parameters could later be put on the population metric through a linear transformation. One limitation to the sampling is that the examinee sample does need to span the range of item difficulties for accurate estimation (calibration) of the item parameters. If an item is very easy or very difficult for a sample of examinees, it is difficult to estimate *how* easy or difficult it is. In other words, the b-parameter will have a large standard error. In Chapter 1, the standard error of θ, called the *standard error of measurement*, was explained. Each of the item parameters also has a standard error—the standard deviation of the estimates of the parameter if it were estimated repeatedly with different random samples of data. The standard error of b depends both on how many examinees were used in the estimation and on how close their θ values were to the location of the b-parameter. Item parameters have information functions just like θs do, although unless otherwise stated the term *information function* can be assumed to refer to information as a function of θ.

The standard error of b will be smaller (information will be larger) when there are more examinees with θ values near b. The a-parameter is estimated best when there is a range of θ values among the examinees. Just as it would be difficult to estimate a regression line accurately if all of the data points were bunched together, it is difficult to estimate the a-parameter without a range of θ values. For the c-parameter, it is particularly important to have examinees with θ values in the range at which the ICC flattens out and approaches the lower asymptote. Otherwise, it is difficult to know whether the item is easy or "easy to guess" (Patz & Junker, 1999, p. 354). For this reason, items that are easy for a sample, or items that are not very discriminating, can often be fit well with either a two-parameter logistic (2PL) or three-parameter logistic (3PL) model (Wells & Bolt, 2008; Yen 1981), but if the wrong model is used it may not fit well in a sample or population with lower θs. Thus, although the sample does not need to be random, the θs in the sample need to cover a broad range. Over-representation of high and low θs might be ideal for accurate parameter estimations, as long as the parameters could be scaled to a random sample from the population to give the metric of the parameters meaning in the population. However, very skewed distributions can increase the standard errors of the item parameters (Sass, Schmitt, & Walker, 2008).

The metric of the item parameters and θs is indeterminant. The center point and the unit size must be fixed. Typically, this is done by fixing the mean θ to 0 and the standard deviation of the θs to 1 in some population of interest, such as a norming sample. If the sample used to calibrate the items is a convenience sample or is intentionally selected to overrepresent the lowest and highest θ values, the resulting metric is not very meaningful. The exception is the *Rasch metric*, where traditionally the center point is set by fixing the mean item difficulty to 0 (thus leaving the mean θ as a free parameter to be estimated) and the a-parameter to 1 (thus leaving the variance of the θs as a free parameter to be estimated). With this scaling, the metric depends on the items but not on the examinees, if population invariance holds.

As discussed, if the parameters are population-invariant; they can be estimated using different samples and will differ only by a linear transformation and random error. However, item parameters very well may *not* be population-invariant. As with any models, there is nothing magical about IRT modeling that will make the parameters population-invariant. For example, Cook, Eignor, and Taft (1988) found that the item parameter estimates for an SAT test in biology depended on how recently the students had completely the biology course. If the items had been population-invariant, the relative difficulty of the items would have remained constant across group. In this context, this was false for *both* the CTT and IRT item difficulties.

Data Requirements

Large samples of examinees are required to accurately estimate the IRT item parameters, and longer tests provide more accurate θ estimates. To a lesser extent, increasing the test length can also improve the accuracy of the item parameter estimation. This results from either improved estimation of the θs or improved estimation of the shape of the θ distribution. In addition, increasing the number of examinees can somewhat improve the estimation of θ through improved estimation of the item parameters.[1]

Turning first to the items parameters, the *b*-parameter is easiest to estimate. Rasch or one-parameter logistic (1PL) models are often used with samples as small as 100 or 200 examinees. Sample size requirements for the *a*- and *c*-parameters depend somewhat on the estimation method (estimation is discussed in Chapter 4). With the estimation method currently used most often for the 2PL and 3PL models (marginal maximum likelihood [MML], often with Bayesian priors), the *a*-parameter generally seems to be well estimated with samples of 500 or even fewer if the items are of moderate difficulty and the θs are normally distributed (see Drasgow, 1989; Harwell & Janosky, 1991; or Stone, 1992 for more specific findings). Reasonably accurate estimation of the *c*-parameter requires larger samples than are needed for the *a* and *b* parameters, and inaccurate estimation of the *c*-parameter can bias the estimation of the *a* and *b* parameters. The accuracy of the estimation of the 3PL ICC as a whole improves noticeably as sample size increases to 2,000, but does not necessarily improve much with samples as large as 4,000 (Woods, 2008b). The

---

[1] Estimation is covered in Chapter 4, and the relationship between the accuracy of θ-estimation and accuracy of item-parameter estimation is explained there.

c-parameter can be difficult to estimate for easy or less-discriminating items (Gao & Chen, 2005; Mislevy, 1986; Patz & Junker, 1999), so sometimes the c-parameter is fixed to a constant value or constrained to a reasonable range of values. It is difficult to recommend specific sample sizes needed to estimate the c-parameter; if the standard error seems large for an item's c, either the sample size should be increased or some constraints should be added, as discussed in Chapter 4. In general, I recommend samples of at least 1,000 to estimate the c-parameter, with the caution that for some of the easier or less-discriminating items the c-parameter may have to be fixed rather than estimated.

Because larger samples are needed to estimate models with more parameters, with small samples more parsimonious models (the 1PL instead of the 2PL or the 2PL instead of the 3PL) may produce more stable parameters, although those parameters may be systematically biased.[2] For example, Lord (1980, p. 190) suggested that the 1PL model might be more accurate with small samples, even when it was not the model underlying the data. Sometimes with small samples the a-parameter or c-parameter are fixed or constrained to have a small variance to avoid estimation problems (Barnes & Wise, 1991; Parshall, Kromrey, Chason, & Yi, 1997).

Using an older estimation technique (joint maximum likelihood, [JML]), the number of items had a larger impact on the estimation of item parameters, and test lengths of at least 40 (Wingersky, 1983) or 60 (Hulin, Lissak, & Drasgow, 1982) were recommended for accurate estimation of the 3PL model. The test length has a lesser impact on item parameter estimation when using the currently popular MML procedure (Drasgow, 1989; Stone, 1992). Fifteen to twenty items appears to be acceptable for item parameter estimation, although more items might be needed to obtain θ estimates with small standard errors, as discussed later in this section. Also, if the θ distribution is skewed, more items,

---

[2] For example, when 3PL data are fit with a 2PL model the a- and b-parameters are underestimated (Yen, 1981). If the estimation samples are randomly drawn from a single population, this effect will be systematic, so that the estimates will be stable from sample to sample—they will be wrong in a consistent way. If the estimation samples represent populations with different ability distributions, in contrast, the underestimation of the a- and b-parameters will vary and the estimates will show greater variance.

perhaps at least 40, are needed even for MML estimation. With smaller numbers of items, the θ distribution is not estimated as accurately, which can in turn impact the estimation of the item parameters (Woods, 2008b).

For polytomous models, the number of examinees per category can make a difference in the accuracy of the category parameter estimation (DeMars, 2003a), and the thresholds are more accurately estimated for middle categories than for extreme categories (Reise & Yu, 1990). The category parameters are also estimated better when examinees are distributed more evenly across categories (de Ayala & Sava-Bolesta, 1999). For the partial-credit model (polytomous Rasch model), Choi, Cook, and Dodd (1997) found that samples as small as 250 appear adequate for three-category items, but samples may need to include 1,000 examinees to accurately recover the step difficulties for the more extreme categories of six-category items. For the Graded Response (GR) model, Reise and Yu's (1990) findings suggested a minimum of 500 examinees, with the error continuing to decrease for even larger samples. The Generalized Partial Credit (GPC) model has the same number of parameters as the GR model, so similar sample sizes would likely be required. All of these recommendations are based on MML estimation.

The accuracy of estimating θ increases with the number of items (as well as the nearness of the item difficulty to the θ location). The number of items necessary to estimate θ well can vary, depending on the match of the item difficulty to θ and on the item discrimination. Better-quality items will be more discriminating and more useful for estimating θ. In short, the number of items needed depends on the information functions of those items, so general rules are difficult to formulate. The information function may be estimated for an existing pool of items, and then items may be added to attempt to increase the information at selected points. The accuracy of the item parameter estimates obviously has some impact on θ estimation as well, so increasing the examinee sample size and thus increasing the item parameter accuracy can increase the precision of θ estimation. However, this effect is small (Choi, Cook, & Dodd, 1997; Reise & Yu, 1990).

In summary, for a 2PL model or 3PL model with fixed c-parameters, if the θ distribution is reasonably normal and the items are highly discriminating, samples of 500 examinees and 20 items would likely be adequate for estimating both item parameters and θs. Minimum samples of at least 1,000 examinees and 40 items would be a more cautious guideline for situations in which the θ distribution may not be normal or the items may not be very discriminating, or if the c-parameter is estimated rather than fixed or tightly constrained. Increasing the sample size and number of items will decrease the standard errors of the parameter estimates, although the increase may be negligible beyond about 2,000–3,000 examinees or 50–80 items.

One additional note on data requirements: IRT models in no way assume a normal distribution. The estimation procedures do not require any assumption of normally distributed examinee ability or normally distributed item parameters. The standard errors of the estimated θ and item parameters are asymptotically normal, but the examinees and item parameters do not need to follow a normal distribution. Severely non-normal distributions may present some practical problems to estimation, as discussed earlier, but this is not due to model assumptions.

Assumptions

Chapter 3 will provide an in-depth discussion of the following three statistical assumptions:

- *Unidimensionality*. All of the models discussed in this book only include a single dimension (θ), so the models are based on the assumption of unidimensionality. Multidimensional IRT models are outside the scope of this book.
- *Local independence*. If the correct dimensionality of the data is specified in the model, the responses to one item will be independent of the responses to another item, conditional on (controlling for) θ. In other words, the correlations among pairs of items are due only to the primary trait or ability measured by the set of test items and are not influenced by some unmodeled trait or ability that impacts both items.
- *Correct model specification*. The data follow the model used in the analysis, such as the 1PL, 2PL, 3PL, GPC or GR models.

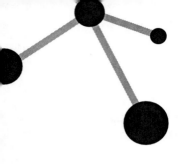

3

ASSUMPTIONS

IN CHAPTER 2, three assumptions of item response theory (IRT) were introduced: unidimensionality, local independence, and correct model specification. In this chapter, each of these assumptions is described more fully, with a focus on procedures for testing each assumption.

Unidimensionality

A test that is unidimensional consists of items that tap into only one dimension. Whenever only a single score is reported for a test, there is an implicit assumption that the items share a common primary construct. Multidimensional IRT models exist, but they are not addressed here. Unidimensionality means that the model has a single θ for each examinee, and any other factors affecting the item response are treated as random error or nuisance dimensions unique to that item and not shared by other items. Violating this assumption may lead to misestimation of parameters or standard errors.

One caution concerning unidimensionality: sometimes test responses can be mathematically unidimensional even when the items measure what psychologists or educators would conceptualize as two different constructs. For example, test items may measure both knowledge and test-taking motivation. Or, items on a science test may measure both reading and science. Or, items may measure both test-taking speed and knowledge. If all items measure both constructs in the same relative proportion, then mathematically they will measure a single θ that is a hybrid of both constructs (Reckase, Ackerman, & Carlson, 1988). Further, if examinees do not vary on one of the constructs, all individual differences will be due to the other construct, and the responses will be mathematically unidimensional. For the test responses to be multidimensional, different items have to tap into different combinations of the constructs, and examinees have to vary on both constructs. In the example here, if some items need lots of motivation but only moderate levels of knowledge (they take some perseverance to work through, but are not difficult if the examinee takes the time to do the work) and other items take little motivation but a high level of knowledge (an examinee either knows the answer or not), then the test will likely not be unidimensional, as long as examinees vary on both motivation and knowledge. If all examinees are sufficiently motivated, motivation will no longer be a factor, and the test responses will be unidimensional (assuming the knowledge measured is unidimensional). For another example, when a test has restrictive time limits even though its intended purpose is to measure content knowledge, the items at the end of the test may measure the construct of test-taking speed more than the items at the beginning, creating multidimensionality. If the test were administered to a group of examinees who were all relatively quick at responding to test items, the test would be more unidimensional. In short, dimensionality may be context- and sample-dependent.

Many methods have been proposed for testing unidimensionality. Hattie (1984) compared 87 methods. More recently, Tate (2003) compared nine of the most commonly used methods. Three common methods are discussed here: analysis of the eigenvalues of the inter-item correlation matrix, Stout's test of essential unidimensionality, and indices based on the residuals from a unidimensional solution.

Eigenvalues

One simple method of testing unidimensionality is based on the *eigenvalues* (roots) of the inter-item correlation matrix. This technique, however, was developed under the assumption of continuous variables. The categories of the items used in IRT are discrete (often dichotomous), not continuous. One problem with this approach with dichotomous data is that *difficulty factors* may be associated with large eigenvalues. This means that items of similar difficulty tend to have high loadings on the same factor. This is particularly likely to occur when the ϕ correlation matrix is analyzed (when Pearson correlations are calculated for pairs of dichotomous variables, they are often called ϕ *correlations*—the terms are equivalent). To mitigate this problem, tetrachoric (or polychoric for polytomous items) correlations are often used in place of the ϕ correlations. However, when the item responses follow a model with a non-zero lower asymptote, such as the three-parameter logistic (3PL) IRT model, analysis of the tetrachoric correlation matrix also can produce difficulty factors and often yields matrices that are nonpositive definite (Hattie, Krakowski, Rogers, & Swaminathan, 1996; Nandakumar & Stout, 1993). Further, tetrachoric correlations are appropriate when the underlying variable is continuous and normally distributed but the observed variable (correct or incorrect response) is dichotomous. This assumption is the same as described for the biserial correlation in Chapter 1: recall that normality is not an assumption of IRT, so this is a stronger assumption than needed for IRT analysis.

Research on using eigenvalues of the correlation matrix to judge dimensionality for dichotomous responses has yielded mixed results. One commonly used way of judging the number of dimensions is to plot the first few ordered eigenvalues (Fig. 3.1), called a *scree plot* because the eigenvalues trail off like the scree (loose rock) at the foot of a mountain. One looks for a steep drop followed by a leveling-off in the values: the number of eigenvalues before the drop represents the dimensionality. In Figure 3.1, there is one eigenvalue before the drop, so we would conclude that there is one dominant dimension. Examining results using this method, Hambleton and Rovinelli (1986) concluded that scree plots of eigenvalues of either the ϕ or tetrachoric matrices were likely to evidence too many factors. In contrast, with de Ayala and Hertzog's (1991) data sets, examination of scree plots and other indices (including percent of common variance accounted for and magnitude of factor loadings) based on either type of correlations accurately identified the number of factors when the correlation between the traits was low. When factors were more highly correlated ($r = .60$), too few, not too many, factors were likely to be retained. In other contexts, with continuous variables, Zwick and

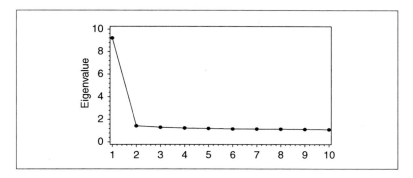

Figure 3.1. Scree plot. The scree clearly begins at the second eigenvalue.

Velicer (1986) describe the scree test as "generally accurate but variable" (p. 432). When in error, use of the scree test tended to overestimate the number of dimensions. Zwick and Velicer's results likely generalize to polytomous items with at least five categories, because ordered responses approach a continuous metric as the number of categories increases.

To describe the scree plot in Figure 3.1, the following explanation could be included in the report, along with the plot:

To assess the dimensionality of the data, a scree plot of the eigenvalues of the tetrachoric correlation matrix was graphed. The scree plot appeared to show one dominant factor, so the assumption of unidimensionality was deemed reasonable.

Often, the point at which the scree begins is more equivocal. If that is the case, a sample write-up might be:

To assess the dimensionality of the data, a scree plot of the eigenvalues of the tetrachoric correlation matrix was graphed. There was a big drop between the first and second eigenvalues, but there was another, smaller drop between the second and third eigenvalues, and again between the third and fourth eigenvalues, before leveling off. This could be interpreted as either one or three factors. There seems to be one dominant factor and two smaller factors.

Note that there is no statistical test to report. If there were a statistical test, the assumption would be met if we failed to reject the null hypothesis. This language should be avoided here because the scree plot is a heuristic procedure used to make a judgment about whether the responses are reasonably unidimensional; it is not a statistical hypothesis-testing procedure.

Another common rule, sometimes implemented by default in statistical software, is to retain factors or components with eigenvalues greater than 1. Reckase (1979) examined this rule for a few simulated data sets, and its use tended to retain extra factors with either the ϕ or tetrachoric correlation matrix. This is not surprising, given that studies in other contexts have generally found this rule leads to the identification of too many factors. Zwick and Velicer (1986) reached this conclusion and cited several studies with similar findings.[1] An examination of the scree plot is likely to be more helpful than retaining dimensions with eigenvalues greater than 1. Although the number of large eigenvalues on the scree plot is often debatable, if the plot clearly shows one eigenvalue before the scree, it seems reasonable to conclude there is likely one dominant factor, or, as in de Ayala and Hertzog's (1991) study, correlated dimensions that might conceptually represent one dimension.

Only a brief summary of the use of eigenvalues for assessing dimensionality has been provided here. The reader is encouraged to reference other texts dedicated to factor analysis to learn more about this particular method.

Other methods for testing the dimensionality of the responses will give more definitive (less subjective) results than methods based on the eigenvalues of the inter-item correlation matrix. Two of these methods will be discussed next.

---

[1] However, Zwick and Velicer (1986) reported more positive results for another method based on the magnitude of the eigenvalues: parallel analysis. Parallel analysis involves comparing the eigenvalues to those from a simulated data set. For continuous variables, Zwick and Velicer (1986) found this to be more accurate than scree plots or the eigenvalue $>$ 1 rule, and Drasgow and Lissak (1983) have applied a modified version to dichotomous items.

Stout's Test of Essential Unidimensionality

Another frequently used procedure is Stout's test of essential unidimensionality (Stout, 1987). It is sometimes simply labeled the DIMTEST procedure because it can be calculated using the DIMTEST 2.0 (Stout, 2005) software for dichotomous items or the POLY-DIMTEST (Stout, 1999) software for polytomous items. Although I have tried to avoid citing specific software in this book, in this case the procedure is often synonymous with the software name. This method provides a statistical test of the null hypothesis of essential unidimensionality. Essential unidimensionality holds when the mean absolute value of the pairwise item covariances, conditional on θ, is approximately 0 (Stout, 1987). This definition highlights the relationship between local independence and unidimensionality. Note the phrase "conditional on θ" in this definition. In the population, the pairwise item covariances should be high and positive if the scores are measuring a meaningful construct. But for examinees with the exact same level of that construct, the pairwise item covariances should be near 0. After controlling for the construct, only random error remains, and these errors are uncorrelated if the test is essentially unidimensional. The θ is not necessarily the IRT θ; it is used here as a generic symbol for the underlying trait, and Stout's procedure does not assume an IRT model underlies the data.

To perform the test, the items are divided into two subtests that are as dimensionally distinct as possible, the Partitioning Subtest and the Assessment Subtest. The Assessment Subtest is composed of items that potentially measure a secondary dimension. This dimension might be identified based on item content. If there is no conceptual or theoretical reason to propose which items might form a secondary dimension, empirical methods can be used to find the best candidate for a possible secondary dimension. DIMTEST 2.0 (Stout, 2005) will optionally use a clustering algorithm to find a secondary dimension, and an earlier version optionally used factor analysis of the tetrachoric correlation matrix. If the items for the secondary dimension are selected empirically, different subsets of examinees should be used to select the items and to perform the dimensionality test, to avoid overcapitalizing on chance (Stout, 1987). After the items for the possible secondary dimension are identified, examinees are grouped by the raw score on the remaining items, the Partitioning Subtest, to calculate the test of unidimensionality. In essence, the procedure tests whether the sum of the pairwise item covariances within score groups is near 0. The number correct on the Partitioning Subtest is used as an estimate of the value on the primary trait measured by the test. Because examinees within each group have the same estimated score on the primary dimension, the covariances between items on the assessment subtest should be near 0 if these items do not share a secondary dimension. After correction for bias, the test statistic, T, is assumed normally distributed. The null hypothesis for T is that the responses are unidimensional (the average covariance within groups $= 0$), so failure to reject the null hypothesis indicates that the assumption of unidimensionality is tenable.

To describe nonsignificant test results, the following explanation could be included in the report:

Stout's test of essential unidimensionality, implemented in DIMTEST 2.0 (Stout, 2005), was used to test the assumption of unidimensionality. Items that might form a secondary dimension, the Assessment Subtest, were selected empirically, using the HCA/ CCPROX cluster procedure and DETECT statistic in DIMTEST, and this candidate cluster was tested to see if it was dimensionally distinct from the remainder of the test. A random sample of 30% of the examinees was used to select the Assessment Subtest, and the remaining sample was used for the dimensionality test. $T = 0.386$ ($p = .3562$, one-tailed); therefore the assumption of unidimensionality was not rejected.

When unidimensionality is not rejected, if the items for the Assessment Test were chosen by empirical methods rather than based on content, there is no need to report which items formed the secondary dimension because the dimension was likely formed by chance. If the items for the Assessment Test were chosen based on content, the report should include a description of why this subset was suspected of possibly tapping a secondary dimension.

To describe significant test results, the following explanation could be included in the report:

Stout's test of essential unidimensionality, implemented in DIMTEST 2.0 (Stout, 2005), was used to test the assumption of unidimensionality. Using a sample of 30% of the examinees, items 3, 8, 15, and 28 were empirically identified by the HCA/CCPROX cluster procedure as the cluster most likely to form a secondary dimension. Using the remainder of the sample for the test of essential unidimensionality, $T = 2.538$ ($p = .0056$, one-tailed), so the assumption of unidimensionality was rejected. Consideration of the content of items 3, 8, 15, and 28 suggested these items could be dropped without appreciably changing the content of the test. When the remaining items were tested, again choosing candidate secondary clusters empirically with a sub-sample of the examinees, the results were not statistically significant ($T = .8957$, $p = .1852$), thus the assumption of unidimensionality was not rejected. Remaining analyses were conducted on this unidimensional set of items.

If unidimensionality is rejected, the report should detail what decision was made and why. If the secondary dimension has many items, perhaps two separate subscales could be formed or a multidimensional model, outside the scope of this book, could be used. If the secondary dimension has only a few items, perhaps those items could be dropped. Or, if those items appear to measure a desired dimension of the construct, perhaps enough similar items could be added to create a reliable subscale. The reader can judge the reasonableness of the decision if the rationale for it is described.

Analysis of Residuals from a Unidimensional Model

Another set of methods in current use involves analysis of the residuals of the bivariate proportion-correct matrix from a unidimensional IRT model. These methods do not seem to be in widespread practical use at the time of this writing, but they are included here because they are currently the subject of much research and may be used more frequently in the future. In Stout's procedure, the primary dimension was held constant by grouping examinees on Partitioning Subtest number-correct scores. In this alternative procedure, the residuals are instead based on the matrix of residual proportions from an IRT model.[2] For an item, the residual proportion correct is the observed proportion minus the proportion expected from the model—these values are the diagonal elements of the matrix. For a pair of items, the residual is the proportion of examinees who answered *both* items correctly, minus the proportion predicted by the model—these values are the off-diagonal elements of the matrix. Under the assumption of unidimensionality, the predicted bivariate proportion correct is the product of the predicted proportion correct for each item in the pair. Typically, the model-based proportions are estimated by integrating $P(\theta)$ across the estimated θ distribution. More simply, this could be conceptualized for a large sample as estimating θ for each examinee, calculating $P(\theta)$ based on the estimated item parameters, and averaging $P(\theta)$ across examinees. After the residual difference between the observed and predicted bivariate proportion correct is calculated, the residual correlation can then be calculated from these residual proportions (see Finch & Habing, 2007, for more details). The residual bivariate–proportion-correct matrix is provided by one IRT program, NOHARM 3 (Fraser & McDonald, 2003). Thus, sometimes these residual analyses are referred to as *NOHARM-based methods*, just as Stout's procedure is sometimes called the DIMTEST procedure after the software that calculates it. The residuals could instead be calculated based on the item parameter estimates from any IRT software, although this would take some additional work.

Several indices based on the residual correlations or residual proportions (covariances) have been proposed. Gessaroli and De Champlain (1996) suggested a χ^2 index based on the squared residual correlations. For data generated to fit the two-parameter logistics (2PL) model, this index had type I error rates below the nominal α. The power rates for rejecting unidimensionality for two uncorrelated dimensions were higher than the power rates for

---

[2] To date, this procedure has only been used with dichotomous items. Item means or a series of submatrices of proportions for each item category would have to be substituted to generalize this to polytomous items.

Stout's procedure when the tests were short. Results were comparable to those of Stout's procedure when the tests were long. Another index, T_s (which is completely unrelated to the T in Stout's procedure), is based on the squared residual proportions (Maydeu-Olivares, 2001) and can be scaled to follow an approximate χ^2 distribution. Finch and Habing (2007) compared Gessaroli and De Champlain's χ^2, T_s, a log-likelihood-type χ^2 index based on the residual proportions, and Stout's procedure. When the data followed a 2PL model, all of these indices had acceptable type I error rates and roughly equal power. But when the data followed a 3PL model, only Stout's procedure and T_s had type I error rates near the nominal α. For the other two measures, type I error rates were inflated more for longer tests and larger sample sizes.[3] Computing T_s is complicated, and this index is unlikely to be included in a test development report. If there is unlikely to be guessing in the responses, perhaps for a constructed-response test or a noncognitive instrument, the simpler Gessaroli and De Champlain χ^2 index might be provided. Although this index is not in widespread use, it was described here because this type of index has been the focus of a number of recent articles and conference papers. Perhaps after the distributional properties are better known, either this type of index may be more widely used in the future or it may be rejected as ineffective. To describe this χ^2 test, the following explanation could be included in the report:

To test the unidimensionality of the item responses, a unidimensional 2PL model was estimated using NOHARM 3 (Fraser & McDonald, 2003). Gessaroli and De Champlain's (1996) χ^2 index was calculated. The test was not statistically significant ($\chi^2_{1222} = 1280$, $p = .121$), so the assumption of unidimensionality was not rejected.

---

[3] De Champlain (1999), using 3PL data, found type I errors for the χ^2 index below the nominal α for sample sizes of 250 or 500, but approaching and perhaps exceeding the nominal α for sample sizes of 1,000. De Champlain's largest sample size, 1,000, was the same as Finch and Habing's smallest sample. De Champlain's type I error rate was somewhat lower, but with only 100 replications, the rate was not estimated very precisely.

Local Independence

Another assumption of IRT is local independence. If the item responses are not locally independent under a unidimensional model, another dimension must be causing the dependence. With tests of local independence, however, the focus is on dependencies among pairs of items. These dependencies might not emerge as separate dimensions, unless they influenced a larger group of items, and thus might not be detectable by tests of unidimensionality. Consequently, separate procedures have been developed to detect local dependencies.

If items are locally independent, they will be uncorrelated after conditioning on θ. Again, note that the items can (and should) be correlated in the sample as a whole. It is only after controlling for θ that we assume they are uncorrelated. Yen (1984) proposed a simple test, Q_3, to check pairs of items for local dependence. First, the item parameters and person parameters for a one-dimensional IRT model are estimated. The model can be the one-parameter logistic (1PL), 2PL, or 3PL model for dichotomous items, or the Graded Response (GR), Partial Credit (PC), or Generalized Partial Credit (GPC) model for polytomous items—whichever model will be used in the rest of the analyses. Based on these item parameter estimates, a residual is calculated for each person's response to each item. The residual is the difference between the predicted item response and the observed response. For dichotomous items, $e = P(\theta) - u$, where e is the residual; $P(\theta)$ is the probability of correct response, given the estimated item parameters and estimated θ; and u is the observed response (0 or 1). For polytomous items, the predicted item score replaces the probability of correct response, and the observed response may cover a larger range. After calculating the residuals, Q_3 is computed as the linear correlation between the residuals from item i and the residuals from item j. The correlation matrix is then examined to find pairs of items with large residual correlations. Yen (1993) focused on the effect size (the correlation) rather than statistical significance (with the large sample sizes used in IRT, a correlation large enough to cause concern would also be statistically significant, as would many correlations not large enough to cause concern). She suggested that test developers focus on correlations greater than .20 as problematic (p. 211).

Notice that the tests for unidimensionality (Stout's procedure and the residual analysis tests) and this test for local independence both center on residual (conditional) covariances or correlations. However, the tests for unidimensionality focus on the sum or average, whereas Yen's test for local independence focuses on individual item pairs. Two items that violate local independence may not be enough to form another dimension, so Yen's test would be more powerful than tests for undimensionality. However, a subset of items may form a secondary dimension without having any pairs of items with correlations large enough to be flagged by Yen's procedure. Thus, unidimensionality and local independence are often tested separately. Local dependency may be a concern when one item builds on the answer to a previous item, or when items are grouped around a reading passage or a common scenario that provides context for all of the items. The violation of local independence in such a case might also be detectable by a test for unidimensionality, but the secondary dimension would be viewed as a nuisance dimension or simply shared error because it is not substantively meaningful.

If a pair of items (or a small group of items) have a large residual correlation, then test developers could choose to drop one of the items from the test, combine the items into a single item, or use a testlet model that allows for small groups of items to measure secondary dimensions. Summing the items is an approach that may be applied to either classical test theory (CTT) or IRT[4]; Yen (1993) illustrated this approach. Instead of two dichotomous items, the sum would be a single polytomous item with 0, 1, or 2 points. The GR or GPC model could be used to estimate the parameters for this item. A small amount of information is lost, because these models do not take into account the different ways an examinee could score 1 point, but the dependency is eliminated. Alternatively, if several items in a subset have elevated residual correlations, the testlet model (Wainer, Bradlow, & Wang, 2007; Wainer & Wang, 2000) can be used. The testlet model essentially includes a shared error term for each small set

---

[4] Correlated residuals can be a problem in CTT, too, because they can lead to misestimation of reliability (Sireci, Thissen, & Wainer, 1991).

of items, which allows the reliability and parameters for the primary dimension to be estimated more accurately.

To describe the Q_3 test, the following explanation could be included in the report:

Yen's Q_3 (1984) was used to check for any large violations of local independence. After controlling for θ, a group of three items had pairwise residual correlations near or greater than .2. The residual correlations were .34 between items 11 and 12, .28 between items 11 and 13, and .19 between items 12 and 13. These items were all centered around a short description of a basketball game and may have inadvertently tapped into basketball familiarity, as well as the intended mathematics construct. These three items were summed and treated as a single item worth 3 points. The GPC model was used to model the responses to this summed item in the remainder of the analyses.

Additional indices have been proposed for testing local independence (for example, Chen & Thissen, 1997, examined four indices). Q_3 is one of the more commonly used.

Fit

The fit between the model and the data can be assessed to check for model misspecifications. For example, if a 1PL model is used and the data follow a model with varying slopes or a non-zero lower asymptote, then many of the items will not fit the 1PL model. If the function is not monotonically increasing, none of the common models will fit. Typically, IRT practitioners focus on the fit of individual items, not the overall fit of the model across all items, which will only be addressed briefly at the end of this section. For item fit, the concept of a *residual*, or the difference between an observed and model-predicted (expected) proportion is key. This residual is conditional on θ, meaning it is calculated for groups of examinees with approximately the same θ. Figure 3.2 shows an item characteristic curve (ICC); the ICC represents the model expectation. Each dot represents a large group of examinees with similar estimated θ. If the model fits, the observed proportion correct

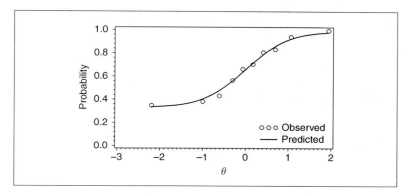

Figure 3.2. Data that fit the model well. The observed proportion-correct values, calculated for sets of examinees grouped by θ level, are close to the ICC.

in each θ-group should be close to the model expectation. The residual is the vertical distance from the observed proportion to the expected proportion, just as in linear regression the residual is the vertical distance between the regression line (expected score) and observed score. Figure 3.3 shows another plot, with somewhat more misfit.

For polytomous items, there are two ways the residuals could be calculated and graphed. The residual could be calculated for each category separately; the plot for category k would show the predicted proportion of examinees choosing/scoring k as a function of θ (the option response function) and the observed proportion

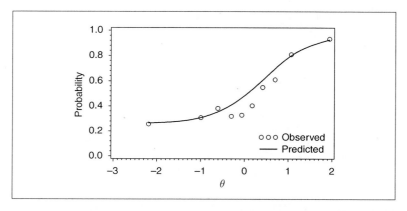

Figure 3.3. Somewhat misfitting data. The observed proportions deviate more from the ICC than the observed values in Figure 3.2 did.

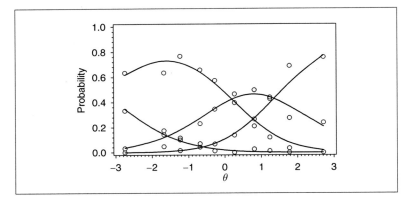

Figure 3.4. Fit of each category for a polytomous item. The open circles indicate observed proportions.

in each θ group choosing/scoring k. An example is shown in Figure 3.4. The solid lines show the predicted probabilities, and the open circles show the observed proportions. Alternatively, the residual could be calculated as the difference between the predicted mean score (the item response function) and the observed mean score for each θ group, as illustrated in Figure 3.5. The latter plot is easier to examine, but it provides less information about which categories misfit. For both dichotomous and polytomous items, examining these plots is a very helpful method for analyzing fit. Indices that summarize the fit are also available.

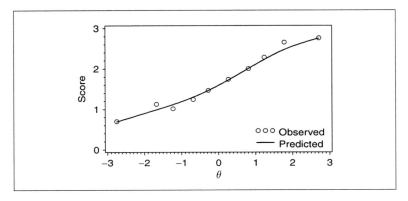

Figure 3.5. Fit of the mean item score for a polytomous item. Observed and predicted scores have been summed over score categories to simplify the graph.

The χ^2 indices used to summarize fit fall into two classes: Pearson χ^2 or log-likelihood χ^2, often symbolized G^2 to avoid confusion with Pearson χ^2. Bock (1972) and Yen (1981) suggested Pearson-type χ^2 indices; Yen's index was labeled Q_1. Examinees are grouped based on estimated θ, and within each group the difference between the observed and expected score is squared and divided by its variance. These terms are then summed across score groups. The observed and expected proportions for polytomous items are calculated within each category and then summed across categories as well as score groups. G^2 is similar, except that the quantities involved are the natural logs of the expected and observed proportions. G^2 is part of the output of BILOG (Zimowski, Muraki, Mislevy, & Bock, 2003) and PARSCALE (Muraki & Bock, 2003). These indices might be expected to follow a χ^2 distribution. However, with large samples and short tests, they can have inflated type I errors (Glas & Suárez Falcón, 2003; Orlando & Thissen, 2000; Orlando & Thissen, 2003; Reise, 1990; Sinharay & Lu, 2008; Wells & Bolt, 2008), especially for polytomous items (DeMars, 2005; Kang & Chen, 2008; Liang & Wells, 2007; Stone & Hansen, 2000). Thus, many items may be falsely rejected as misfitting, which would waste good items and increase test development costs.

One reason for the inflated type I error rate is that θ may not be well-estimated, especially for short tests. Orlando and Thissen (2000; 2003) and Stone (2000) proposed different approaches to address this problem. Orlando and Thissen (2000) developed modified χ^2 and G^2 indices, labeled S-χ^2 and S-G^2, for dichotomous items. They grouped examinees based on observed number-correct score, not on θ. Although calculating the expected item score for a particular θ is straightforward when given the item parameters, calculating the expected item score for a particular number-correct score is not. Each possible score pattern that sums to score X corresponds to a different likelihood function for θ, so these functions must be summed across score patterns. After multiplying the resulting likelihood function by the density of θ, the expected (mean) θ for examinees with score X can be computed and in turn used to compute the expected item score. Orlando and Thissen (2000) described an algorithm for these calculations. With samples of 1,000, S-χ^2 maintained an empirical type I error rate near the nominal rate (Orlando &

Thissen, 2000). S-G^2 showed a somewhat inflated error rate, but not nearly as bad as the unmodified version for short tests. For a very long test (80 items), S-G^2 did not improve much over the unmodified version, although with the long test even the unmodified version rejected at a rate of only two to three times the nominal α (compared to nearly 100% false rejection for a 10-item test). However, Glas and Suárez Falcón (2003) found comparable performance for S-χ^2 and S-G^2. In their studies, both indices rejected too often with very large samples of 4,000, or even samples of 1,000 when the test was short (10 items). Despite this, the modified indices performed much better than the unmodified versions. Additionally, these indices have been extended to polytomous items. For the GPC model and restricted versions of the GPC model, Kang and Chen (2008) found S-χ^2 controlled the type I error rate accurately for most sample sizes and test lengths, whereas the unmodified G^2 had inflated type I error for short tests, especially with large samples.

Another approach, developed by Stone (2000; 2003; Stone & Hansen, 2000), is to avoid assigning each examinee to a single θ group. Instead, each examinee is assigned fractionally to each level of θ proportional to the likelihood of θ given the examinee's response pattern. When the standard error of θ is small (reliability is high), the examinee may weight mostly in one θ group, perhaps 90% in one group, 5% in each of the adjacent groups, and approaching 0% along the rest of the distribution. But when the standard error of θ is big (reliability is low), there is less confidence about the examinee's θ, and the examinee's weights are spread out over a broader range of θ, reflecting that uncertainty. Once these weights are estimated, the χ^2 or G^2 are calculated. These indices are distributed as scaled-χ^2. Stone (2000) provided methods for calculating the scaling constant and modified degrees of freedom. Using data that followed the 2PL or graded-response model, Stone (2003) found type I error rates close to the nominal rates, even with short tests (6 or 12 items) and large samples (2,000). Additionally, Sinharay and Lu (2008) studied Stone's procedure with 3PL data and found inflated type I error rates with large samples ($N = 2,000$). This finding suggests that this procedure may control type I error rates much better when the true underlying model has a lower asymptote of 0 (2PL or most polytomous models).

A different approach was taken by Douglas and Cohen (2001) and Wells and Bolt (2008) for dichotomous items and Li and Wells (2006) and Liang and Wells (2007) for polytomous items. They compared the ICC to a nonparametric ICC, which is basically a smoothed line connecting the observed score-proportions for the θ groups. Finding the probability values for each item requires *bootstrapping procedures* (simulating a distribution using the estimated item parameters). Additionally, other item fit indices or modifications have been developed (for example: Donoghue & Humbo, 2003; Glas & Suárez Falcón, 2003). Because most of these indices are not in widespread use, it is important to include information about the properties of whichever index is chosen, such as type I error and power to detect particular types of misfit.

Given the inflated type I error rate of the unmodified χ^2 and G^2, especially with large sample sizes and short tests, the modified indices are more appropriate if statistical significance testing is desired. But if the focus is on effect size (how badly does the item misfit?), a visual inspection of the residual plot, as shown in Figure 3.2, may be adequate. Although a visual inspection does not give a statistical test of fit, it may be enough to make a determination of whether the model fits reasonably well. As Lord (1968) noted, "The appropriate question is not whether the model holds exactly—this can hardly be expected—but whether it can provide trustworthy approximate answers to important questions" (p. 990). An example write-up of this simple approach follows:

The log-likelihood fit index, G^2, was obtained from BILOG-MG (Zimowski, Muraki, Mislevy, & Bock, 2003), along with item parameter estimates. Two items had large G^2 indices, suggesting they may not fit the model well. Because G^2 sometimes has a high type I error rate, plots of the observed and predicted responses (ICC) were examined. These plots are provided in Figures 3.2 and 3.3. The item in Figure 3.2 appears to fit reasonably well and was left in the item pool. The item in Figure 3.3 shows an unusual pattern, with examinees of moderate proficiency scoring unexpectedly low. This item will be referred to content experts for possible explanation of the misfit and revision of the item.

One additional note: because the type I error rate of the unmodified χ^2 and G^2 is high for large samples, it might be tempting to conduct fit tests with a smaller subset of the sample. This would be problematic because the item parameter estimates would be less accurate (higher standard errors) and the residual plots would have more error as well.

Users of Rasch models apply different fit indices than do users of IRT models. For two common indices, instead of grouping examinees, a residual is calculated for each examinee: the difference between the observed response (0/1 for dichotomous items, or item score for polytomous items) and the model-predicted response ($P(\theta)$ for dichotomous items). The residual is standardized by dividing it by its standard deviation. The squared standardized residuals can be averaged over persons, for item fit, or over items, for person fit (Wright & Masters, 1982, Chapter 5). Outfit mean square (MS) is an unweighted average of the squared standardized residuals. For Infit MS, the squared standardized residuals are weighted by the variance (equivalent to summing the squared unstandardized residuals). Infit is less sensitive to residuals from people whose abilities are far from the item difficulty. Infit MS and Outfit MS are *not* distributed as χ^2, but they can be transformed to a t-distribution for statistical testing (Wright & Masters, 1982, Chapter 5). Others use Infit/Outfit MS as effect sizes: items are flagged if Infit/Outfit MS is greater than 1.5 (or < 0.6; sometimes other cut-offs are used, such as 1.3, in part depending on the proposed use of the score and type of item (Engelhard, 1992; Linacre, 2006; Wright & Linacre, 1994). Wilson (2005, Chapter 6) recommended using the statistical test and examining MS effect sizes for the statistically significant items, as is done in many areas of statistics. This does not seem to be frequent practice; a choice between statistical significance and effect sizes appears to be more common among Rasch model users (for example, Smith, Schumacker, & Bush, 1998).

Rasch model users also frequently focus on person fit. The Infit and Outfit indices can be calculated for each examinee by summing the squared weighted or unweighted residuals across items, within an examinee. Linacre (2006) provides explanations for common patterns of misfit, such as fatigue effects. Misfitting examinees can be removed before recalibrating the item parameters, and the scores of misfitting examinees may be flagged as invalid. This is a fairly typical part of Rasch modeling. Many person-fit indices have been proposed for IRT or CTT analysis as well (for example, see Karabatsos, 2003, for a description of 36 different indices). However, they are typically used in an effort to detect a particular type of misfitting response, such as cheating or responding randomly. Person fit generally is not a routine step in IRT analysis as it is in Rasch modeling, but perhaps more accurate item parameters could be estimated if the data were screened for misfitting examinees.

Finally, the overall fit of the model could be considered instead of or in addition to item fit. Overall model fit is not nearly as commonly reported as item fit. One straightforward procedure is to compare the observed total score distribution to the model-predicted score distribution (Swaminathan, Hambleton, & Rogers, 2007). The distributions could be visually compared or the difference between them could be assessed with a statistical test such as the χ^2 test. Tests are also available for comparing the fit of different models. When maximum likelihood estimations procedures are used, a model deviance index can be calculated to compare two nested models. For each model, −2 times the natural log of the overall likelihood of the observed response patterns, given the estimated item parameters and the estimated θ distribution (for short, the log-likelihood)[5] is calculated. When models are nested, the difference between their −2 log-likelihoods is theoretically distributed as χ^2 with degrees of freedom equal to the number of additional item parameters in the larger model. This is sometimes called a *likelihood ratio test*—the log of the ratios of the squared likelihoods is the same as 2 times the difference in the log-likelihoods. Models are nested when one model is a special case of the other model, with some parameters constrained to be equal to each other or to zero. For example, the 1PL model is nested within the 2PL model because all *a*-parameters are constrained to be equal. The 2PL is nested within the 3PL because all *c*-parameters are constrained to be zero. The PC model is nested within the GPC

---

[5] When marginal maximum likelihood is used, the likelihood of each response pattern is integrated over the θ distribution, so the likelihood is conditional on the estimated θ distribution, not on the individual θ estimates. Under direct maximum likelihood, the likelihood would be conditional on both the estimated item parameters and the θ estimates.

model. But the PC model is not nested within the GR model. The PC model has fewer parameters to be estimated than the GR model, but it is of a completely different functional type so it is not nested.

Although use of the difference in log-likelihoods to compare nested models has been described for IRT (Embretson & Reise, 2000, Chapter 9; Thissen, Steinberg, & Gerrard, 1986), it does not seem to be widespread, and its properties do not seem to have been explored in detail. Kang, Cohen, and Sung (2005) found this index was accurate for identifying whether data were generated from the GPC, PC, or rating scale model. For dichotomous models, Kang and Cohen (2007) found that this index yielded correct decisions for 1PL and 2PL data, but 3PL data appeared to fit the 2PL model when the test was relatively easy compared to the θ distribution.[6] For comparing unidimensional and two-dimensional IRT models, this test seems to have inflated type I error rates for the 3PL model (De Champlain & Gessaroli, 1998; DeMars, 2003b). However, this is a different application than comparing nested unidimensional models, so the results may not generalize.

Other indices of overall model fit have been proposed to compare non-nested models. Again none of these indices is in widespread use. Maydeu-Olivares, Drasgow, and Mead (1994) used the ratio of the likelihoods of the data under different models to compare the fit of the GR and GPC models, and found that the GPC and GR models often fit the data about equally well regardless of which model was used to generate the data. Kang and Cohen (2007) and Kang, Cohen, and Sung (2005) used two indices based on the likelihood (AIC and BIC).[7] In their 2005 study, data generated to fit the GPC model fit the GPC model better than the GR model, but data generated to fit the GR model was also

---

[6] This can be true for item fit as well. Using Q_1, Yen (1981) showed that easy items tended to fit the 2PL model because there were few examinees in the region where the non-zero lower asymptote determined the ICC. Using the 2PL, the a-parameters were underestimated, so that the ICC could slope less steeply and reach down to a lower asymptote of 0. Wells and Bolt (2008) showed that easy or less-discriminating 3PL items tended to fit the 2PL well. Mislevy (1986) also discussed this "trade-off" between item parameter estimates, but in the context of parameter estimation, not item fit.

[7] They also compared two indices based on Markov chain Monte Carlo (MCMC) estimation, which will not be discussed here because these indices are even less likely to be encountered in routine reports.

identified as better fitting the GPC model when the item threshold distribution did not match the θ distribution well. The 2007 study involved dichotomous items. Like the test for the difference in log-likelihoods, the AIC and BIC were accurate when the data were generated by the 1PL or 2PL, but they tended to identify the 2PL model for 3PL data when the test was relatively easy (BIC tended to select the 2PL model in all conditions).

In short, comparison of the fit of non-nested models, like comparison of the fit of nested models, needs more research before it becomes routine. Overall model fit might seem to be a reasonable consideration when two models are under considera-tion, but more often the models are selected based on other considerations, as described in Chapter 1, where the most com-monly used models were introduced. The content and purpose of the test should be considered when choosing reasonable models (Kang & Cohen, 2007; Thissen, Steinberg, & Gerrard, 1986).

If two models fit the data equally well, it might seem to be a matter of indifference which is chosen. The problem is that the model fit may be population-specific. For dichotomous items, Yen (1981) suggested that selecting the 2PL model when the data were generated under a 3PL model yielded item parameters that might not generalize to a less-able or more-able population. The a-parameter and b-parameter estimates of the 2PL are adjusted to take into account any data at the low end of the distribution (low relative to the item difficulty), so that the proportion of examinees in the lower range impacts how much these parameters are mis-estimated. Additionally, because using the wrong model affected the more difficult items more than the easier items, the correlation between the true and estimated 2PL a-parameters was relatively low in Yen's study, and the 2PL a- and b-parameters were nega-tively correlated. Similarly, Bolt (2002) showed that GR item parameters could be selected to fit GPC data well in a particular population. However, they were not invariant to the population; in a less-able or more-able population, different GR item parameters would better fit the GPC data. The problem is that using the wrong model does make a difference if the item parameters will be used for populations that vary in mean θ, but this is difficult to detect when data are only available from one population. Additionally, when the shape of the population distribution is estimated empirically along with the item parameters (see Chapter 4), misspecification of the model may be compensated for by errors in the estimation of the population distribution, so that the wrong model appears to fit well (Woods, 2008a).

Chapter Summary

In this chapter, three assumptions of IRT analysis have been described: unidimensionality, local independence, and correct model specification. Some of the many tests for these assumptions have been explained. For each assumption, a number of statistical tests have been proposed and explored in the literature. Only a few of these could be detailed here. Weaknesses of some common approaches and indices have been noted, and newer alternative procedures have been described. Unfortunately, some of these procedures are quite complex and not easily implemented.

Chapter 4 returns to the questions posed at the beginning of Chapter 2. Most of these questions can be addressed by examining the item or θ parameters, so the chapter begins with an explanation of parameter estimation.

4

RESULTS

THIS CHAPTER returns to a discussion of the research questions noted at the beginning of Chapter 2. Each of the questions is addressed in turn, with an explanation of how the output can be used to find answers. Most of the questions relate to the item or examinee parameter estimates. Before examining how the questions can be answered, the next section gives a brief, conceptual explanation of how the parameters are estimated.

Estimation

Estimation of θ

The simplest case occurs when the item parameters have been estimated in a previous sample and are used to estimate an individual examinee's θ score or the θ-distribution of a group of examinees. This would be the case for on-demand testing, in which examinees take the test at different times and receive a score immediately. It would also be the case for standardized tests in which all of the operational items have been calibrated previously in another sample(s). Score estimation utilizes the likelihood function. For an item, the likelihood function for a correct response is $P(\theta)$, the item characteristic curve (ICC) discussed in Chapter 1 (see Figures 1.2–1.7, in this volume). The likelihood function for an incorrect response is $1 - P(\theta)$, producing a backward "S" shape. The likelihood function for an examinee's response pattern for all of the items on the test is the product of the response patterns for the individual items, due to the assumption of local independence. Figure 4.1 shows the individual item likelihood functions for six item responses with the pattern 111100. Figure 4.2 shows the likelihood function for the entire pattern. The maximum likelihood

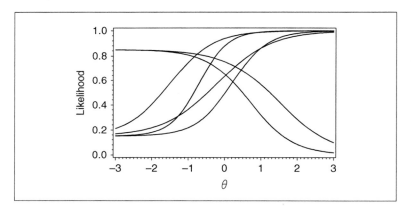

Figure 4.1. Likelihood for 6 item responses (111100), as a function of θ. As θ increases, the likelihood of each of the 4 correct responses increases but the likelihood of each of the 2 incorrect responses decreases.

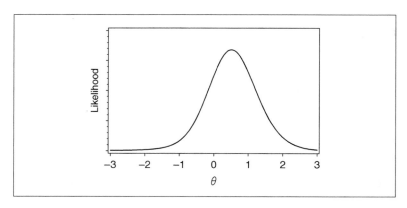

Figure 4.2. Joint likelihood of the response pattern 111100.

(ML) estimate of θ is the θ value at which the likelihood function reaches a maximum. In Figure 4.2, the ML estimate of θ would be 0.5. Notice that the focus is on the *relative* value of the likelihood, to find the θ that corresponds to the maximum value. The numerical value of the likelihood is of little concern. In fact, as more items are added to the test, the likelihood for any one response pattern gets smaller and smaller. But the maximum value becomes much larger *relative* to the remainder of the function. The maximum could be found by using a grid search, evaluating the function at intervals of, for example, 0.01. With modern computers, this would not be very time-consuming. However, the maximum can be found even faster using calculus. Most item response theory (IRT) programs use the Newton-Raphson procedure (described briefly in the Appendix to this chapter).

Sometimes it is useful to consider information about how θ is distributed in the population, called the *prior* distribution. For example, if the ML estimate of θ for a response pattern is −5, this is a very unlikely value if the examinee is a member of a population that is approximately normally distributed with a mean of 0 and standard deviation of 1. It would be reasonable to adjust the estimate of θ for this response pattern a little closer to the mean. Additionally, if an examinee answers all the items correctly (or incorrectly), the likelihood function continually increases with θ and never reaches a defined maximum. In this case, it would be practical to obtain an estimate above the population mean but within a reasonable range. The use of a prior distribution can help in these cases. In Bayesian statistics, the prior distribution is multiplied by the likelihood function based on the observed data. The product is called the *posterior* likelihood.[1] Figure 4.3 shows the posterior likelihood for a standard normal prior multiplied by the likelihood in Figure 4.2. Notice that the location of the maximum is a bit closer to 0, and the dispersion of the likelihood is somewhat less (which indicates a smaller standard error). To estimate θ, we can either find the maximum of this function or the mean. The θ estimates based on the maximum are often called *modal-a-posterior* (MAP) estimates because the function

---

[1] The posterior distribution is rescaled to have a density of 1. The posterior distribution can be interpreted as the likelihood of θ, given the data and the prior distribution. The likelihood function, in contrast, is the likelihood of the data given θ, which is less intuitively useful for estimating θ.

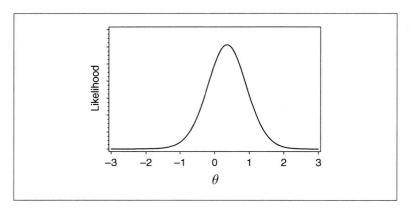

Figure 4.3. Posterior likelihood of θ, given the response pattern 111100 and a standard normal prior distribution. Compared to Figure 4.2, the maximum of the function occurs somewhat closer to $\theta = 0$.

reaches its maximum at the modal value. The mean estimates are often called *expected a-posterior* (EAP) estimates because the *expected value* is a statistical term for the mean over an infinite number of replications. These Bayesian estimates are *biased*, meaning that at a fixed value of θ, the expected value of the estimate does not equal θ. If the true θ is lower than the mean of the prior distribution, the expected value of the estimate is positively biased (i.e., too high), and if the true θ is greater than the mean of the prior, the expected value of the estimate is negatively biased. In other words, the estimate is biased toward the mean of the prior. The more data points (item responses, in this case) that are available for an examinee, the less influence the prior will have. Also, the closer the true θ is to the prior mean, the less biased the estimates will be. Additionally, the use of a prior will produce a likelihood with a defined maximum even when an examinee answers all items correctly (or incorrectly). The standard error of θ will be large for such an examinee because this set of items does not provide much information about precisely how high θ is, but the function will have a maximum.

Often, researchers or policy consumers may be interested in the distribution of θ within a group or subgroup of examinees. When using number-correct scores, the distribution is typically estimated by estimating a score for each examinee and then finding the distribution of these scores, with the distribution usually characterized by the mean and standard deviation of the score estimates. In IRT, the group mean of θ is well estimated by the mean of either the ML or Bayesian (EAP or MAP) estimates. However, the standard deviation of θ is *overestimated* by the standard deviation of the ML estimates and *underestimated* by the standard deviation of the Bayesian estimates.[2] The standard deviation of θ can be estimated directly, *without* estimating the individual θ scores. The details of this procedure are beyond the scope of this book (see Baker & Kim, 2004, Chapter 10, or Mislevy, 1984). The important point here is that directly estimating the standard deviation will be more accurate than indirectly estimating it through the estimates of the individual examinees' scores. The direct estimate of the variance is analogous to true score variance in classical test theory (CTT).

Item Parameter Estimation

Estimating either the θ distribution or the θs for individual examinees is thus fairly straightforward after the items are calibrated. Estimating the item parameters is somewhat more complicated. One of the most common estimation methods for the item parameters is *marginal maximum likelihood* (MML, Bock & Aitkin, 1981).[3] In statistics, the marginal distribution is the distribution of one variable after marginalizing (averaging) over the distribution of another variable. In this case, the marginal likelihood referred to in MML is the likelihood of the item parameters after marginalizing over θ. By marginalizing over the θ distribution, this procedure greatly reduces the number of unknowns to be estimated. The process begins by assuming an initial distribution for θ, usually standard normal.[4] Then, the marginal likelihood of the

---

[2] As discussed, the Bayesian estimates are biased toward the mean, so their standard deviation will be lower than the standard deviation of the true θs.

[3] Wainer, Bradlow, and Wang (2007, p. 84) noted that this procedure is more appropriately labeled *maximum marginal likelihood* because it involves maximizing the marginal likelihood. Both terms are now used in the literature, and they have the same acronym.

[4] This is sometimes called the "prior distribution," because it is assumed *a priori*, without reference to the data. It should not be confused with the prior distribution used in the EAP or MAP estimates—unfortunately, it is the same label for a different concept. It would be less confusing to reserve the term *prior* for the prior distribution of the parameter we are estimating and not for the distribution of the incidental parameters.

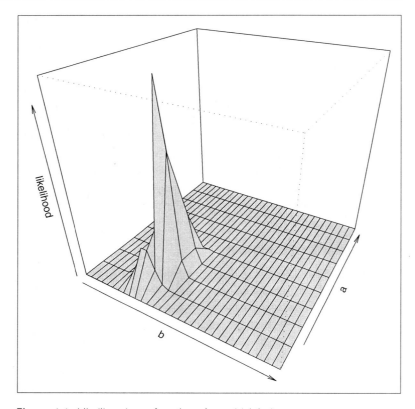

Figure 4.4. Likelihood as a function of *a* and *b* jointly.

item parameters is estimated, given this θ distribution and the item responses. The likelihood function for a two-parameter logistic (2PL) item is shown in Figure 4.4 (the likelihood function for a three-parameter logistic [3PL] item is more difficult to illustrate because it would require a fourth dimension). The object is to find the *a*- and *b*-parameter estimates where the likelihood function reaches a maximum. Because of the assumption of local independence, we can work with the likelihood function for each item separately, just as we could work with the likelihood function for each examinee separately when we were estimating θ. However, within each item *a*, *b*, and *c* are not independent. For example, if *c* is underestimated, *b* will be underestimated (the item will seem easier because guessing is not taken into account) and *a* will be underestimated (the slope will be less steep so that the ICC can approach a smaller lower asymptote). The maximums must be found simultaneously, but sometimes multiple combinations of a, b, and c have similar likelihoods. Prior distributions for the item parameters can be useful in these situations.

Just as Bayesian priors may be used for estimating θ, Bayesian priors may be used for the item parameters. This procedure could be called Bayesian MML or simply MML with priors. The reason for using priors on the item parameters is that, as Mislevy (1986) explained, sometimes very unreasonable values for one parameter, when combined with unusual parameters for the other parameters, can fit the ICC as well as another, more reasonable triplet of parameters. This is because, as described earlier, the parameter estimates within an item are not independent; mis-estimation of one parameter can compensate for mis-estimation of another. Using priors helps avoid very odd sets of item parameters. Priors have the biggest impact on the item parameters when the examinee sample is small (Gao & Chen, 2005). They also have a bigger effect when an item's parameters are far from the mean. When all examinees answer an item correctly (or incorrectly), multiplying the likelihood by a prior will yield a product with a defined maximum, parallel to the context of estimating θ for an examinee who answers all items correctly. Very restrictive priors can be used when little information is available from the data, such as for the c-parameter for easy items.

After the item parameters have been estimated once, the θ distribution can be updated. Either a normal distribution can be assumed, or the distribution can be approximated as a histogram.[5] If the distribution is assumed to be normal, the mean and standard deviation of θ are estimated, given the current item parameter estimates. As described earlier, the mean and standard deviation are estimated directly, not through estimating the individual θs and finding their mean and standard deviation. If the distribution is instead characterized by a histogram, the proportion of the population within each bar of the histogram

---

[5] Other methods for estimating the shape of the θ distribution have been developed, such as the use of Ramsay curves (Woods, 2006), but the histogram method is implemented in commercial software and is easiest to explain.

is estimated (see Baker & Kim, 2004, Chapter 10, or Mislevy, 1984, for details). Then the mean and standard deviation can be found using procedures for grouped data. The mean and standard deviation will likely be slightly off 0 and 1 at this point, so a linear transformation is used to make the mean 0 and the standard deviation 1, and this same transformation is applied to the item parameters. This step is not strictly necessary, but it is the typical way to define the metric. Then the item parameters are reestimated, followed by reestimation of the θ distribution. This continues until any changes in the item parameter estimates meet the convergence criterion, perhaps .01. The final estimate of the θ distribution is called the *posterior distribution*. This should not be confused with the posterior distribution obtained for an examinee by multiplying the examinee's likelihood by the group's distribution. In that context, the group's posterior distribution serves as the examinee's prior distribution. Again, unfortunately, the same label is used.

After the item parameters and the θ distribution have been estimated, the examinees' θs can be estimated through ML, EAP, or MAP estimation. These are not a by-product of the item parameter estimation but a separate step.

An alternative to MML is *joint maximum likelihood* (JML). Joint maximum likelihood uses the individual θ estimates instead of marginalizing over the θ distribution, alternating between item parameter estimation and θ estimation. The θs are thus estimated along with the item parameters, instead of estimated in a separate step afterward. This works very well with the one-parameter logistic (1PL) or Rasch models, and was historically used with the 2PL and 3PL models as well. With JML, because the individual θs are estimated, typically the metric is scaled so that the observed standard deviation of the estimates is 1. Because the variance of the ML estimates tends to overestimate the true variance of θ, the units on the θ metric will be slightly wider. The metric is arbitrary, and this difference is noted here only to alert the reader that the metric will be slightly different depending on whether the items are calibrated through MML or JML procedures.

After estimating (calibrating) the item parameters and the θ distribution and perhaps the examinees' θs, the research questions described in Chapter 2 can be addressed.

Research Questions

What Is the Spread of Item Difficulties (and Category Difficulties, for Polytomous Items)?

The item difficulties can be used to judge whether the test or survey items are targeted to the level of θ where measurement precision is desired. In Chapter 1, the meaning of each of the parameters was described. The values of the item parameters can be used to examine this question. To assess the item difficulty, the b-parameters can be inspected. For the 1PL and 2PL models, the b-parameter is the location at which an examinee has a 50% probability of answering the item correctly, or of endorsing the item. For the 3PL model, the probability is slightly higher than 50%. For all three dichotomous models, the b-parameter is the location at which the probability is changing most rapidly.

The b-parameters, or category thresholds, in the Graded Response (GR) model have a similar interpretation. The threshold for category x is the point at which the examinee has a 50% probability of scoring in category x or higher, and it is also the point at which the probability of category x or higher is changing most rapidly. The b-parameters, or step difficulties, in the Generalized Partial Credit (GPC) model have an entirely *different* interpretation. The step difficulties indicate the location at which the probabilities for adjacent categories intersect. Another way of thinking about it is that the step difficulty is the location at which adjacent categories are equally likely. Conditional on scoring in one of the two categories and no other, the examinee at that point has a 50% probability of scoring in each. If thresholds are transformed to step difficulties, or vice versa, the values of the parameters may be quite different. Thus, they should not be compared unless one set of parameters is first transformed to make them comparable.

Knowing the estimated b-parameters is useful in judging the difficulty or appropriateness of the instrument for a given group. An instrument that is intended to measure θ across a wide range should have a range of b-parameters, perhaps from -2 to 2. To measure equally well at all points, the b-parameters should be uniformly distributed across the desired range, but more often a greater number of middle-difficulty items are selected to measure most of the examinees more precisely while losing some measurement precision for the smaller number of examinees at the extremes. Each polytomous item can measure across a wider range of θ, if the *b*-parameters within the item are spread out. If the *b*-parameters for a polytomous item are in a narrow range, it functions more like a dichotomous item. This idea will be revisited in the information (reliability) section. Sometimes one of the middle categories will contain very few of the examinees. This can happen when the first step of an item is fairly difficult, but the next step is simple once the first step is solved correctly. Or, a rubric category may describe a stage that is possible, but rarely seen. If the GR model is used, the thresholds for the adjacent categories will be very close, and the confidence intervals around the *b*-parameters will likely overlap, suggesting that the categories are indistinguishable. If the GPC (or Partial Credit [PC]) model is used in this situation, a step reversal may result. A step reversal means that the step difficulties are not in sequential order. For example, if the step difficulties were (−0.2, −0.6, 0.3, 1.4), the intersection between scores 1 and 2 would be at a lower θ value than the intersection between scores 0 and 1. Figure 4.5 shows an item with these GPC parameters and *a* = 1. Figure 4.6 shows the closest-fitting GR parameters for this item—notice how the first two thresholds are very close together, corresponding to the step reversal for the GPC parameters, although the steps are not literally reversed using the GR model. Each of these thresholds will have large standard

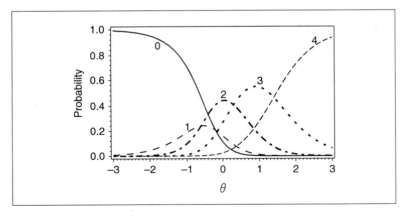

Figure 4.5. GPC item with a step reversal. The second step difficulty (intersection of scores 1 and 2) is located at a lower *θ* than the first step difficulty (intersection of scores 0 and 1).

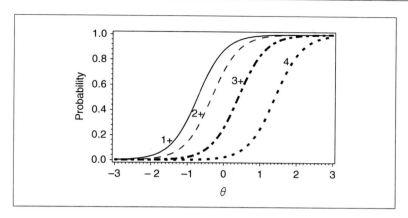

Figure 4.6. GR item corresponding to data in Figure 4.5. The first two thresholds are located close together.

errors because the adjacent categories are difficult to distinguish. Andrich's view (2002) is that step reversals indicate a problem with the scale or the way the respondents or raters are using the scale. The test content experts should examine the item to see if the category causing the reversal is redundant with the next category and make sure it is worded clearly for the respondents or raters.

Figures 4.7 and 4.8 show several dichotomous items, calibrated with the 3PL model. In Figure 4.7, the *b*-parameters are spread out,

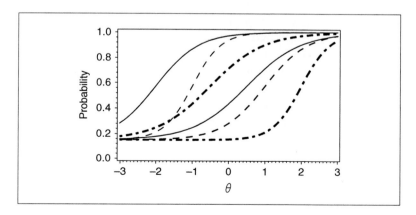

Figure 4.7. ICCs for 6 dichotomous items with difficulties distributed over the θ range. Compare the spread of the functions here to the clustering of the functions in Figure 4.8.

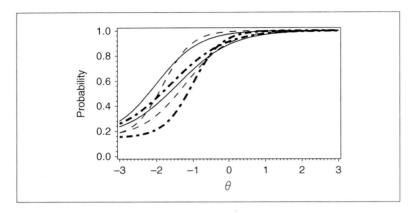

Figure 4.8. ICCs for 6 dichotomous items with difficulties clustered at the low end of the θ range. Due to the small variance in difficulty, the ICCs are located close together.

and in Figure 4.8 the b-parameters are grouped in a narrower range. The wider range would be useful for many achievement tests in which the test user wants to estimate each examinee's θ well. The narrower range might be useful for a test in which the user only wants to know whether the examinee passed or failed. All of the items in Figure 4.8 are easy, so the user can obtain a good measure of what those examinees who are near the low end of the ability continuum know. However, the user can not get a very good idea of what higher-scoring students know—all that can be inferred from the test score is that they know more than the level of items on this test. If the passing score were near the low end of the θ range, this set of items would be useful for determining whether an examinee's θ was above or below the passing score. If the item difficulties were grouped at the other end of the scale, the test would be more useful for high cut-scores, such as a merit scholarship test or a clinical diagnosis that is met by only a small proportion of the population with such a high level of the construct. Low scores could only be used to infer that the examinee or respondent was nowhere near the merit level or clinical diagnosis; they would not tell us more precisely what the examinee knows or how psychologically well the examinee is.

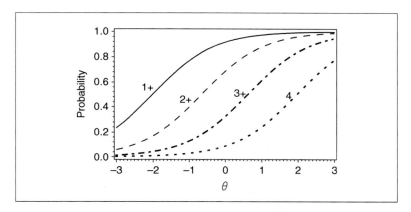

Figure 4.9. Polytomous item with broadly spaced categories.

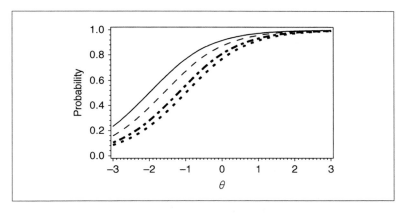

Figure 4.10. Polytomous item with narrowly spaced categories. This item differentiates well only among respondents at the low end of the θ range.

Figures 4.9 and 4.10 each show a polytomous item, calibrated with the GR model. The categories in Figure 4.9 are spread out further, so this item would be more appropriate across a wider range of θ. When the categories are located closer together, as in Figure 4.10, the item is more useful for a narrow range of θ. Each polytomous item in essence functions as a set of dichotomous items, and the categories may be spread out to measure across a wide range or grouped together to measure more precisely in a narrow range.

Standard errors should be reported along with the *b*-parameters. The sampling distribution for each item parameter is asymptotically normal, so 95% confidence intervals can be formed by adding/subtracting 1.96 times the standard error to/from the estimate of the parameter (*a*, *b*, or *c*).

How Discriminating Is Each Item?

The *a*-parameter tells how steep the item slope is, or how rapidly the probability is changing at the item difficulty level. For the 1PL and PC models, the discrimination is assumed to be the same for all items within a test. For the 2PL, 3PL, GR, and GPC models, the items within a test have varying *a*-parameters. As noted in Chapter 1, discrimination is an important attribute. If an item is not very discriminating (low value for the *a*-parameter), then the probability of correct response (or item endorsement) will not increase very much with increasing levels of θ. The item will not help measure the examinee's θ. Figure 4.11 shows an example of a GPC model item with a high *a*-parameter and Figure 4.12 shows an item with a low *a*-parameter. Notice how flat the curves are in Figure 4.12.

With polytomous items, sometimes the term *discrimination* is used to refer not to the item's *a*-parameter but instead to the item's maximum information. Information was introduced briefly in

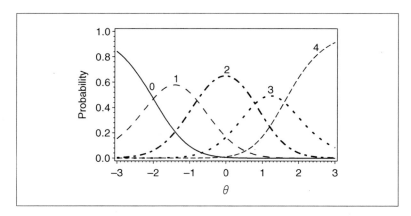

Figure 4.11. Polytomous item with a high *a*-parameter.

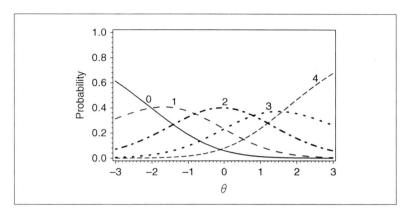

Figure 4.12. Polytomous item with a low *a*-parameter.

Chapter 1 and will be discussed in a later section. The relevant point here is that the maximum information depends not just on the *a*-parameter but also on the spacing of the category parameters.

The next question moves away from the item parameters and focuses on the examinees.

What Is the Distribution Of Abilities/Traits in this Group of Examinees/Respondents? How Does the Ability Distribution Compare to the Item Difficulty Distribution?

As noted at the beginning of this chapter (and in Chapter 1, in this volume), the metric of the measurements must be defined by choosing a center point and a unit size. If the items have not been calibrated (the item parameters have not been estimated) before, then typically, in the calibration sample, the metric is set by defining the θ distribution to have a mean of 0 and standard deviation of 1. If the calibration sample is a meaningful norming sample, this metric will probably be used later to estimate the θs of new examinees to a constant metric. Otherwise, it would be possible to redefine the metric later, but all of the item parameter and θ estimates for the original sample would need to be transformed to the new metric. This is relatively easy because of the property of invariance introduced in Chapter 1. Only a linear transformation (a multiplicative constant and an additive constant) is needed and, as long as the same transformation is applied to both the item and θ estimates, the probability functions will not change.

When the metric is centered on the examinee sample of interest, comparisons between the item parameters and the θ distribution are straightforward because the θ distribution has an estimated mean of 0 and estimated standard deviation of 1. If the θ distribution is more or less normal, even if it is a bit skewed or kurtotic, most of the examinees' θs will be within 2 or 3 units of 0, with a denser distribution near 0 and fewer and fewer examinees at the extremes. Given this, if the mean item difficulty is near 0, the test is well-matched to the examinees' θs. From an examinee perspective, the test might be perceived as quite hard, because the average examinee would have about a 50% probability (a bit more with guessing) of correct response for the average item. But from a measurement perspective, θ and b would be considered well-matched. Similarly, if the b-parameters have a higher mean, the test is difficult; if they have a lower mean, the test is easy for these examinees.

If the difficulties of individual items are of interest, graphical displays can illustrate the relative difficulties. The θ distribution can be plotted on the same graph for comparison. This is routine in Rasch analyses, but it is sometimes used in IRT reports as well. In Rasch analysis, the metric is often centered not around the θs, but around the item difficulties. If the test is easy for the sample of examinees, the mean θ will be greater than zero. If the test is hard for the sample of examinees, the mean θ will be less than zero. If the θ distribution has a large variance, these items discriminate among examinees in this sample well, and, conversely, if the θ distribution has a small variance.[6] Another way of thinking about this is: If the examinees have a large variance, they are more accurately separated (discriminated) from each other than they would be if they had a small variance.

Rasch users produce *item maps* (sometimes called *Wright maps*, Wilson, 2005) to show these relationships. Figure 4.13 shows an

---

[6] Because of the relationship between the a-parameter and the variance of θ, if the variance were greater than 1 and the metric were redefined such that the variance was 1, the transformed a-parameter would then be greater than 1. This is why the mean a-parameter and the variance of θ cannot both be fixed; either one alone sets the unit size.

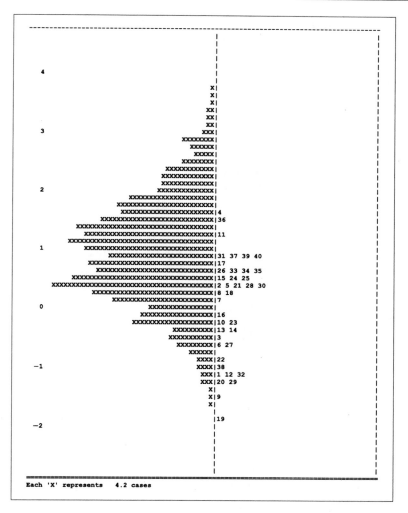

Figure 4.13. Item map. The vertical axis indicates the difficulty or proficiency scale. The left half of the chart depicts the distribution of the examinees, and the right half of the chart shows the item difficulty locations.

item map. The item numbers are plotted on one side, at the values of their item difficulties. The step difficulties could be plotted for polytomous items, indicating step 1 for item 1 with the label 1.1, and so forth. The ability distribution is shown in the other half of the graph. Each X represents a person (or persons). An examinee (or teacher or parent) might want to focus on his or her score value and its relationship to the item difficulties. The examinee likely got most of the items below that value right, and would be quite challenged by most of the items above that value. This could help an examinee decide what to study next. For the sample as a whole, one can look at the distribution of θ and see which items fell toward the low end (most examinees would answer these correctly) and which items fell toward the high end (few examinees would get these right). This could be used to help plan instruction for a group of students or as summative assessment of a group's progress. Another use for Rasch item maps is to examine the order of the item difficulties for validity purposes. If the items have been written based on a construct map (a structured, ordered definition of the skills or theoretical trait intended to be measured by the instrument), the item map should follow the construct map. This can be used as evidence of content validity (Wilson, 2005, Chapter 8). This purpose might be most clear for measures of psychological traits, where there is a strong theory of which characteristics require higher levels of the trait for endorsement.

Item maps can also be created for items calibrated with the 2PL or 3PL models (or the polytomous GR or GPC models). To construct the map, a response probability (RP) must be selected by which to locate the items. Rasch item maps typically map the item by the item's difficulty, which is the location at which the probability of correct response is 50%. If data follow the Rasch model, the order of the items would remain the same if they were mapped to 67% or 75% probability. Only the scale value would change; a constant would be added to each item's location as the chosen response probability increased. But recall that the ICCs for 2PL and 3PL data can cross. For low θs, item 1 might be more difficult than item 2, whereas for high θs, item 2 might be more difficult than item 1. Thus, the choice of the response probability for the item map can make a difference in how the items are ordered. Item response theory users have been criticized by Rasch proponents because the item order depends on the RP chosen. For example, Wilson (2004, p. 137) has criticized the idea behind this process of mapping 2PL or 3PL items to a selected RP, suggesting that this approach ignores the problem of RP-dependent ordering. Item maps are used in some methods of standard setting, so the implications of the RP choice have been described in the standard-setting literature (Beretvas, 2004; Karantonis & Sireci, 2006), as well as in the context of choosing appropriate items for public descriptions of performance levels (Zwick, Senturk, Wang, & Loomis, 2001).

It is important for the documentation to specify the response probability chosen for the mapping. For example, the documentation might say:

In the item map, each item is located at the θ level at which two-thirds of the examinees "know" the item (after correcting for chance guessing). The order of the items roughly corresponds to the order of their b-parameters but may sometimes be inconsistent due to differences in the a-parameters. (The b-parameters are based on the proficiency level at which about 50% of the examinees "know" the item, after correcting for guessing. If an item is very discriminating, the two-thirds location will be reached soon after the b-parameter, but if the item is not very discriminating the two-thirds location may be a long proficiency distance from the b-parameter.)

For many audiences, the explanation of why the item map does not always order items in the same way as the b-parameters would seem excessive. However, if no explanation is included, someone may notice the discrepancy, think it is a mistake, and get side-tracked on this issue. Including an explanation may help prevent this. Of course, if a 1PL or Rasch model were used, the order of the items would be constant regardless of the RP, so this statement and explanation would not be relevant or appropriate.

As with the Rasch item maps, examinees or their parents can compare IRT scores to the item map for feedback on the types of skills they have likely mastered. Policy makers can compare the score distribution to the item map to get a more global view of what students know. For example, the National Assessment of Educational Progress (NAEP) provides item maps and marks the transitions between below basic, basic, proficient, and advanced on the item map (for example, see http://nces.ed.gov/nationsre-portcard/itemmaps). Currently, NAEP uses a 65% response probability for constructed-response items and a 72%–74% response probability for five- or four-option multiple-choice items, which is equivalent to 65% after accounting for guessing, if guessing is assumed to be 1/(number of options).

How Much Information Does the Test Provide over the Ability/Trait Range? How Does Each Item Contribute to the Test Information?

The test information function was described briefly in Chapter 1. It is the sum of the item information functions. Item information depends on the item parameters. For dichotomous items, within an item, the information reaches its highest value at or near where $\theta = b$. The item information is more peaked when the a-parameter is high and flatter when the a-parameter is low. Figure 4.14 shows the information function for two items with the same b-parameter of 0.3, but different a-parameters ($a = 1.2$ for item 1, $a = 0.7$ for item 2). Near $\theta = 0.3$, the more discriminating item has more information, but for θ values further away, the less discriminating item has slightly more information. This is because the ICC for a discriminating item changes rapidly near b but is essentially flat, near 0 or 1, for θs further away. But the probability for a less discriminating item changes more gradually over θ, providing a small amount of information across a broader range. A non-zero value for the c-parameter decreases the information, particularly for low-ability examinees, and shifts the

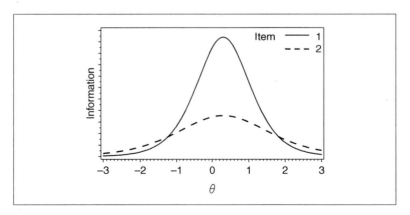

Figure 4.14. Item information functions for items with different a-parameters. For both items, $b = 0.3$, but a is higher for Item 1 than for Item 2.

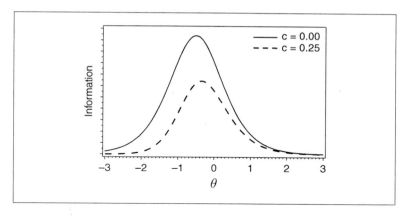

Figure 4.15. Item information functions for an item with $c = 0.00$ and an item with $c = 0.25$. For both items, $a = 1.2$ and $b = -0.5$. Information is lower when c is greater.

point of maximum information a bit above b. Figure 4.15 shows the information for a 2PL item ($a = 1.2$, $b = -0.5$, $c = 0.00$) and a 3PL item ($a = 1.2$, $b = -0.5$, $c = 0.25$).

The information function is the negative of the expected value of the second derivative of the log-likelihood function.[7] For the 3PL model, the item information function is: $I_i(\theta) = 1.7^2 a_i^2 \frac{(1-P_i)(P_i - c_i)^2}{(1 - c_i)^2 P_i}$, which simplifies to $I_i(\theta) = 1.7^2 a_i^2 (1 - P_i)(P_i)$ for the 2PL or 1PL models.

For polytomous items, each category provides information. The item information can be partitioned to obtain the category information share functions. If categories within an item are close together, the item information will be peaked near the center of the b-parameters. But if the categories are spread further apart, each can add information at a different location. Thus, the item information for a polytomous item can have multiple peaks and can be spread over a broader extent of the θ range. Thus, a polytomous item can potentially provide much more information

---

[7] For the 3PL model, the second derivative depends on whether the response was correct/incorrect, so the expectation (average) is taken by weighting the second derivative for a response (0/1) by the probability of that response. For the 1PL and 2PL models, the "expected value" part of the phrase can be dropped because the second derivative does not depend on the response.

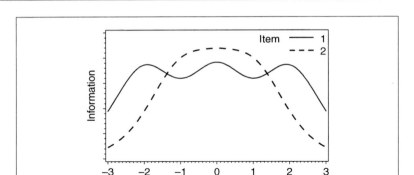

Figure 4.16. Item information functions for polytomous items with different category spacings. The thresholds for Item 1 are spread further apart.

than a dichotomous item. In Figure 4.16, the categories for item 1 are spread further apart than the categories for item 2.

The item information functions can be summed to form the test information function: $I(\theta) = \Sigma I_i(\theta)$. The standard error of measurement (or standard error of θ) for ML scores is the square root of $1/I$ (θ). The information increases additively with each additional item, but the standard error of measurement is not decreased proportionally, because the square root function is a nonlinear transformation. When the standard error of measurement is large, adding another item has a bigger impact than when the standard error of measurement is smaller. This is analogous to CTT; adding an item to a short test has a bigger impact on reliability and standard error of measurement than adding an item to a long test (consider the Spearman-Brown prophecy formula). An information function and the corresponding standard error of measurement function were illustrated earlier in Chapter 1, Figure 1.1 (in this volume). When the information is larger, the standard error of measurement is smaller. Information is thus analogous to reliability, except that it is a function of θ and is applicable to an individual score, whereas reliability is a summary index used for a group of scores.

Like the binomial-based standard error, the IRT standard error of measurement depends on the trait level. However, the IRT standard error is larger for extreme scores while the binomial standard error is smaller for extreme scores. This is because the

IRT scale is infinite. When an examinee or respondent scores high on the instrument, we know that the examinee is high on the trait but we do not have a very precise estimate of how high—it could be considerably higher than the instrument's scale reaches. The number-correct scale, in contrast, is limited to the range between 0 and the maximum score on the test. When the observed score is at the top of the instrument's scale, it would likely remain at the top of the scale over repeated administrations of test forms composed of items drawn randomly from a pool of similar items. Thus, the incongruity is simply a consequence of differences in the number-correct and IRT scale metrics.

When MAP scores are used instead of ML scores, the log of the prior distribution is added to the log-likelihood function and thus the second derivative of the log of the prior is added to the information. If a normal distribution is used as the prior distribution, the second derivative of the log is simply the standard deviation. Thus, a constant equal to 1/variance (often 1) is added to the information function at all levels of θ. MAP scores therefore have slightly more information (and smaller standard errors) than ML scores, especially in regions where the information was lower, because the constant will have a relatively larger impact when information is low. For EAP scores, the standard error is the standard deviation of the examinee's posterior distribution, which can be approximated by the square root of the inverse of the information for MAP scores (Thissen & Orlando, 2001, p. 118). The posterior standard deviation of the EAP score is typically a bit smaller than the square root of the inverse of the MAP information function. They approach equality as the test length increases. Software programs estimate the posterior standard deviation directly, not by approximation through the information function. But the information function is more useful than the posterior standard deviation for test development because it is a direct function of the item parameters.

For a Given Population or Sample Distribution, How Reliable Are the Ability/Trait Estimates?

In many ways, the information and standard error functions are more helpful than a reliability index because these functions provide more detail. The *Standards for Educational and Psychological*

Testing (American Educational Research Association, et al., 1999) recommend reporting conditional standard errors at multiple score levels (Standard 2.14). This is straightforward using IRT. Additionally, the test information, unlike a reliability index, is the sum of the item information and is thus easy to compute for any test form that may be created. However, sometimes test users want a single index instead of a function. Further, the units of reliability are easier to interpret. Reliability can be explained as an estimate of the proportion of variance due to true differences among examinees, not random error. Or, it can be explained as the estimated squared correlation between the score estimates and the true/universe score. With either explanation, the index is on a 0–1 scale, in contrast to the standard errors, which are on the same scale as the θs. Thus, sometimes reliability is estimated for the θs. The reliability is sometimes called the *marginal reliability* (Green, Bock, Humphreys, Linn, & Reckase, 1984) because it is marginalized (averaged) over the θ distribution. Similar indices have also been labeled *theoretical* or *empirical* reliability (Zimowski, Muraki, Mislevy, & Bock, 2003, pp. 33–34). Rasch users typically employ the term *reliability of person separation* (Wright & Masters, 1982, chap. 5) or simply *separation reliability* (Bond & Fox, 2001, Chapter 3; Wilson, 2005, Chapter 7). These seem apt descriptors because reliability is an index of how accurately the scores separate or discriminate among examinees. All of these indices are based on the basic CTT definition of reliability as the ratio of true score variance to observed variance.

Different researchers have proposed different ways of calculating these variance terms, but the results should be very close. The Appendix explains some of the proposed indices. For ML scores, recall that the variance of the estimated scores overestimates the true score variance. Thus, the variance of the score estimates is analogous to observed score variance, and the average squared standard error is the error variance. For Bayesian (EAP or MAP) scores, recall that the variance of the score estimates *under-*estimates the true score variance. Thus, in the reliability formulas used with Bayesian scores, the variance of the score estimates is more analogous to the true score variance, with the observed score variance replaced with either the direct estimate of the θ variance or the variance of the score estimates plus the average squared standard error. (Again, details are available in the Appendix.) With any of these formulas, the estimated reliability of the IRT scores will generally be slightly higher than the estimated reliability of the number-correct scores (for example, coefficient α). The IRT scores are usually more reliable because the score estimation essentially weights more discriminating items more highly. Even in the 1PL model, where all items have equal a-parameters, the IRT reliability may be a bit higher because the scale units are sized more uniformly than the number-correct score (raw-score/observed) units (recall from Chapter 1 that the 1PL scores are not simply a linear transformation of the number-correct scores).

As in CTT, the reliability for IRT scores must be with reference to a particular group of examinees (or more accurately, with reference to a particular score distribution). In both IRT and CTT, if the mean standard error of measurement stays constant but the score variance increases (group heterogeneity), the reliability will increase.

Sample Write-Up: Dichotomous Items

The following write-up describes the results for an analysis of dichotomous items. Comments on the write-up and further explanations are provided following the example report.

Results

The American Experience test was designed to measure university students' knowledge of U.S. history and political science. It had 40 multiple-choice items. Each item had four options and was scored as incorrect (0) or correct (1). A group of 2,692 students participated in the test. Most (70%) of the examinees had completed either a U.S. history course or a political science course at the college level.

The data were checked for unidimensionality to ensure a single score was appropriate. Using DIMTEST 2.0 (Stout, 2005) the assumption of unidimensionality was not rejected. Thus, these data appeared essentially unidimensional. In this procedure, a sample of 30% of the examinees was used to search for clusters of

(continued)

(*continued*)

items that might be influenced by a secondary dimension. The most likely cluster was tested using the remaining examinees, and this cluster did not share a statistically significant secondary dimension ($T = 0.386$, $p = .3562$, one-tailed). Additionally, after the IRT calibration (described next) all pairs of items were checked for local independence using Yen's Q_3 (1984). None of the pairwise residual correlations were greater than .10 in absolute value, which is below Yen's suggested cut-off of .20. Local dependence did not appear to be a problem.

The items were calibrated with a three-parameter logistic (3PL) model. In this model the probability of correct response is modeled by: $P(\theta) = c_i + (1 - c_i)\frac{e^{1.7a_i(\theta - b_i)}}{1 + e^{1.7a_i(\theta - b_i)}}$, where θ is the examinee's demonstrated proficiency in the area of history/political science, a is the item discrimination (also called the item slope), b is the item difficulty, and c is the lower asymptote (the probability that someone with a very low proficiency will answer the item correctly, perhaps by guessing). In this context, the term *proficiency* should not be interpreted as the examinee's true, inner level of knowledge. All that can be measured with the test is the proficiency that the examinee demonstrated on the test, which could be confounded with motivation and situational factors.

The parameters were estimated using maximum marginal likelihood (MML) in BILOG-MG 3 (Zimowski, Muraki, Mislevy, & Bock, 2003). Priors for the item parameters were estimated empirically from the previous step. The proficiency distribution was estimated empirically using 20 quadrature points. The estimation converged after 13 cycles. All items fit the model reasonably well. Using the log-likelihood-ratio χ^2 (G^2) provided in BILOG-MG, item 7 misfit at a .05 α-level ($G^2(9) = 19.4$, $p = .02$). Because 40 items were tested for fit, one or two might be expected to misfit at this level by chance. A plot of the expected and observed values for item 7 is shown in Figure 4.17. The observed probabilities were not far from the expected probabilities, so no further action was taken for this item.

Table 4.1 provides the estimates of the item parameters (standard errors in parentheses).

(*continued*)

(*continued*)

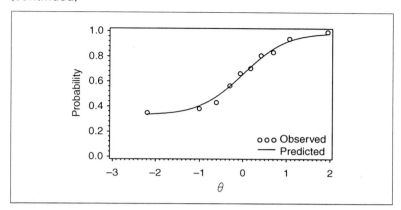

Figure 4.17. Fit for Item 7. This was the worst-fitting item, but the misfit does not appear to be severe.

Table 4.1

Item Parameters

Item	Discrimination	(SE)	Difficulty	(SE)	Asymptote	(SE)
1	0.82	(0.07)	−1.47	(0.14)	0.15	(0.06)
2	0.57	(0.07)	0.11	(0.19)	0.26	(0.06)
3	0.81	(0.08)	−0.75	(0.14)	0.26	(0.06)
4	0.68	(0.09)	1.15	(0.09)	0.15	(0.03)
5	0.69	(0.08)	0.18	(0.14)	0.26	(0.05)
6	0.77	(0.06)	−1.10	(0.12)	0.12	(0.05)
7	1.14	(0.12)	0.00	(0.08)	0.32	(0.03)
8	1.42	(0.14)	0.05	(0.06)	0.28	(0.03)
9	0.79	(0.09)	−1.53	(0.24)	0.37	(0.08)
10	0.59	(0.07)	−0.59	(0.23)	0.28	(0.07)
11	0.79	(0.08)	0.69	(0.07)	0.14	(0.03)
12	0.48	(0.05)	−2.11	(0.30)	0.21	(0.08)
13	0.89	(0.09)	−0.55	(0.13)	0.29	(0.05)
14	0.80	(0.09)	−0.43	(0.16)	0.33	(0.06)
15	0.82	(0.08)	0.15	(0.10)	0.22	(0.04)

(*continued*)

(*continued*)

Table 4.1 (Continued)

Item	Discrimination	(SE)	Difficulty	(SE)	Asymptote	(SE)
16	0.70	(0.08)	−0.45	(0.16)	0.25	(0.06)
17	1.01	(0.11)	0.47	(0.07)	0.25	(0.03)
18	0.60	(0.07)	−0.15	(0.18)	0.24	(0.06)
19	0.83	(0.07)	−2.11	(0.16)	0.14	(0.06)
20	0.64	(0.05)	−1.87	(0.22)	0.19	(0.08)
21	0.82	(0.08)	−0.01	(0.10)	0.21	(0.04)
22	0.76	(0.07)	−1.12	(0.17)	0.25	(0.07)
23	0.89	(0.08)	−0.62	(0.11)	0.20	(0.05)
24	0.95	(0.09)	0.01	(0.08)	0.19	(0.04)
25	0.69	(0.07)	0.08	(0.13)	0.23	(0.04)
26	0.74	(0.07)	0.05	(0.10)	0.15	(0.04)
27	0.75	(0.07)	−0.92	(0.16)	0.23	(0.06)
28	0.77	(0.08)	−0.03	(0.11)	0.21	(0.04)
29	1.07	(0.08)	−1.31	(0.11)	0.17	(0.05)
30	0.75	(0.08)	−0.04	(0.12)	0.23	(0.04)
31	0.56	(0.06)	0.38	(0.14)	0.15	(0.04)
32	0.71	(0.06)	−1.58	(0.20)	0.21	(0.07)
33	0.68	(0.08)	0.29	(0.13)	0.23	(0.04)
34	0.90	(0.08)	0.07	(0.08)	0.15	(0.03)
35	0.82	(0.07)	0.01	(0.08)	0.12	(0.03)
36	0.90	(0.11)	0.99	(0.07)	0.18	(0.02)
37	0.62	(0.08)	0.68	(0.13)	0.24	(0.04)
38	0.46	(0.04)	−2.06	(0.28)	0.18	(0.08)
39	0.54	(0.07)	0.44	(0.15)	0.17	(0.05)
40	0.67	(0.09)	0.68	(0.12)	0.26	(0.04)

For item discrimination, a higher value indicates that the item discriminates (differentiates) between high and low proficiency examinees better. For this test, the highest discrimination was

(*continued*)

(*continued*)

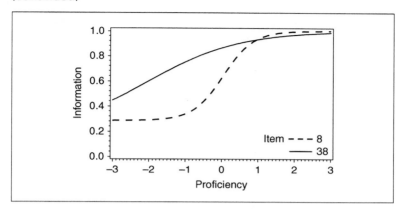

Figure 4.18. ICCs for the most and least discriminating items on the test. Performance on Item 8, the most discriminating item, increases rapidly as proficiency increases.

1.42 for item 8, and the lowest discrimination was 0.46 for item 38. The item characteristic curves (ICCs) for these two items are shown in Figure 4.18. In this graph, proficiency on the test runs along the x-axis (the horizontal axis). The average proficiency was set to 0, with a standard deviation of 1. Approximately 95% of the examinees' proficiency scores were between –2 and 2. When an item has a high discrimination, high-proficiency examinees have a much higher probability of answering it correctly than low-proficiency examinees. Thus, the ICC curves in a sharp 'S' shape, as for item 8 in Figure 4.18. A less-discriminating item, such as item 38, slopes more gradually. In other words, the performance of low-ability and high-ability students is not very different. A low-discriminating item thus does not give as much information about an examinee's proficiency. Similar graphs are available for all items in the Appendix to this report. Items 2, 12, 31, 38, and 39 were the least discriminating.

The item difficulty column indicates how easy or hard the item was for these students. Easier items have lower (negative) difficulty indices and harder items have higher (positive) indices. On this test, item 12 was the easiest item and item 4 was the hardest. Items 12, 19, 20, and 38 were so easy that nearly all examinees chose the correct answer.

(*continued*)

(*continued*)

The lower asymptote represents the proportion of very-low-proficiency examinees who would get the item correct. For example, about 15% of very low proficiency examinees would be predicted to choose the right answer for item 1. Because these are multiple-choice items, this could be due to random guessing. To decrease the possibility of random guessing, distractors (wrong answers) that are appealing to low-proficiency examinees could be designed. This would only be effective for examinees who read the item and attempt to choose the most reasonable response.

The standard error for each parameter estimate conveys the degree of estimation precision. For example, the standard error of the difficulty estimate was high for item 12. This was a very easy item, so it was hard to estimate precisely *how* easy it was.

The distribution of examinees' demonstrated proficiencies was also estimated. A graph of the distribution is shown in Figure 4.19. Notice that there is a heavier lower tail than would be expected in a normal distribution. In this low-stakes context, this may be due to examinees who obtained very low scores because they were not bothering to read the question or response options. The mean proficiency was set to 0, and the standard deviation of the proficiency scores was set to 1. This determined the metric of the item parameters reported in Table 4.1. For an item with a difficulty parameter near 0, such as item 7, after discounting guessing about 50% of this group of students answered the item correctly. The item difficulties in Table 4.1 can be compared to the proficiency distribution; at the point where the difficulty matches proficiency, a little more than half of the examinees at that proficiency answered the item correctly. Among the examinees above that proficiency level, a greater proportion answered the item correctly.

A proficiency score was estimated for each individual examinee as well, using maximum likelihood estimation. It is important to know how precisely the proficiency scores are estimated. The information function indicates the precision of the proficiency estimates. The square-root of the inverse of the

(*continued*)

(*continued*)

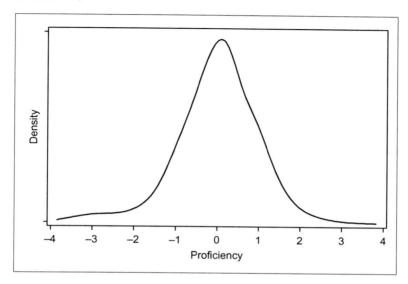

Figure 4.19. Estimated distribution of proficiency.

information function is the standard error of the proficiency score. The information function and standard error are plotted in Figure 4.20. Notice that there is more information, and thus smaller standard errors, for middle ranges of proficiency. The information function is the sum of the item information functions. Each item gives more information near its difficulty parameter than at proficiencies further from its difficulty. Items with higher discrimination indices give more information. In Figure 4.21, the information function is plotted for the two items whose ICCs were previously shown in Figure 4.18. Notice that item 8 gives more information than item 38. Also, item 38's information peaks at a much lower proficiency level because it is an easier item than item 8. Information functions for other items are provided in the Appendix.

An average index of reliability can be based on the mean standard error. As in classical test theory, the reliability can be calculated as: (observed variance − error variance)/(observed variance). For this group, the average reliability was .87.

(*continued*)

(*continued*)

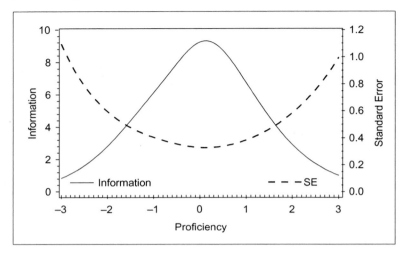

Figure 4.20. Test information and standard error of the proficiency estimates.

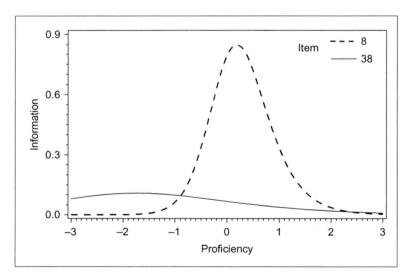

Figure 4.21. Item information functions for Items 8 and 38. Information is greater for the more discriminating Item 8.

(*continued*)

(*continued*)

In summary, these test items were well-matched to these students' proficiencies, and the maximum likelihood proficiency estimates were reasonably reliable. Items 2, 12, 31, 38, and 39 contributed less than the other items to the information (reliability) because they were not very discriminating, and items 12, 19, 20, and 38 did not add much information because they were very easy. These items might be considered for deletion or replacement.

Comments on the Write-Up

This write-up began with some background on the test. The amount of background needed will depend on the audience, but it should at a minimum include information on the number of items, the test format, and the data sample used for the item calibration.

This write-up was addressed to an audience that knows nothing about IRT. If one can assume that the reader knows IRT, one can simply note that the 3PL model was used and skip an explanation of the model and the parameters. The estimation procedure was noted, even though it was not explained, partly to maintain thorough documentation for future reference, and partly in case the reader knows enough about IRT to question the parameter estimation. The software used was noted, not to advocate a particular package, but because estimation procedures vary depending on the software and version. Referencing the software thus gives the reader additional details about the estimation. This is not necessary for basic statistical procedures that will not vary with the software, such as a *t*-test, but is important for more complicated procedures.

In some cases, the θs might be transformed to avoid negative scores. If a transformation is applied to the θs, the same transformation should be applied to the item parameters. For example, if the θs are multiplied by 100 and a constant of 500 is added, so that the scale has a mean of 500 and standard deviation of 100, the *a*-parameters must be divided by 100 and the *b*-parameters must be multiplied by 100 and a constant of 500 must be added. This was avoided in the sample write-up to prevent confusing readers who are just becoming comfortable with the usual IRT scale, but in some reports it may be preferable.

Instead of using the symbol θ, the term *proficiency* was used throughout this write-up. This was a test of knowledge, so labels like *ability* or *proficiency* are more appropriate than *trait*. Ability is somewhat more likely than proficiency to be misinterpreted as the examinee's exact knowledge state that we could measure under ideal conditions. This misinterpretation might also apply to *proficiency*, so the phrase *demonstrated proficiency* was used and defined in the beginning to better convey the idea that θ is simply the knowledge that the examinee showed on one occasion, and it is bound together with such things as motivation and temporary mood or physical states. Remember, as long as these attributes are relatively constant throughout the test, in a mathematical sense they are not separate dimensions but are instead bundled together with θ and will not emerge as a separate factor in the dimensionality analyses.

The write-up referred to an appendix with the ICCs and information functions. To save space, this appendix was not provided here.

Sample Write-Up: Polytomous Items

The next write-up describes the results for an analysis of polytomous items. Again, comments and further explanations are provided following the example report.

Results

The Motive to Avoid Failure scale (Hagtvet & Benson, 1997) was administered to 2,747 incoming first-year university students. This instrument has six items with four response options: *Almost Never*, *Sometimes*, *Often*, and *Almost Always*. It is intended to measure students' fear of failure and discomfort with working in situations where success is uncertain.

The eigenvalues of the correlation matrix were extracted for a rough check on the assumption of unidimensionality. The ordered eigenvalues were 3.53, 0.74, 0.68, 0.46, 0.40, and 0.36. The big drop between the first and second eigenvalue, followed

(continued)

(*continued*)

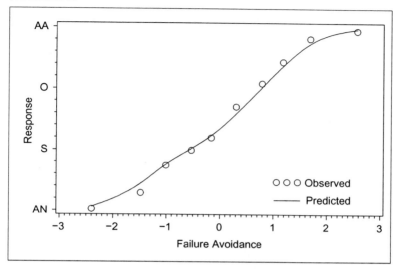

Figure 4.22. Item fit for Item 2. The misfit does not appear to be severe. AN = almost never, S = sometimes, O = often, AA = almost always.

by a leveling off of the remaining eigenvalues, suggested there was one dominant dimension. More rigorous tests of dimensionality were not practical due to the short test length.

The items were calibrated with a graded response model using MML estimation in PARSCALE 2.0 (Muraki & Bock, 2003). The item fit index G^2 available in this software has an extremely high false rejection rate with short instruments and large samples, so, not surprisingly, the fit of each item was rejected at the .01 level using this index. Instead of relying on this index, fit was judged by examining the plot of expected and observed scores. This plot is shown for the worst-fitting item, item 2, in Figure 4.22 and for the other items in the Appendix. The line shows the expected response from 0 (*Almost Never*) to 3 (*Almost Always*) as a function of Motivation to avoid failure. Respondents were grouped into 10 levels of failure avoidance; the open circle indicates the observed average response for each group. The observed responses seem to fit the model predictions reasonably well; the biggest difference was for the second-lowest group, where respondents chose lower

(*continued*)

(*continued*)

(almost never) responses somewhat less often than predicted by the model. The moderate to high groups chose slightly higher levels of endorsement than predicted by the model. Overall, model fit appeared adequate.

Table 4.2

Graded Response Parameters

Item	Slope	SE	Threshold for S	SE	Threshold for O	SE	Threshold for AA	SE
1	0.75	0.02	−3.08	0.09	−0.05	0.04	1.65	0.05
2	1.16	0.02	−2.04	0.05	−0.12	0.03	1.24	0.04
3	1.05	0.02	−1.48	0.04	0.81	0.04	2.25	0.06
4	1.41	0.03	−0.81	0.03	0.81	0.03	2.00	0.05
5	1.76	0.04	−1.27	0.03	0.57	0.03	1.76	0.04
6	1.54	0.03	−1.37	0.03	0.27	0.03	1.26	0.03

Note: S = Sometimes, O = often, AA = Almost Always

Table 4.2 shows the estimated item parameters. The *slope* is an index of how rapidly the response probability changes as failure avoidance increases. The *thresholds* each indicate the point at which 50% of respondents would choose the designated option or higher. Everyone has a 100% probability of choosing *Almost Never* or higher, so there is no threshold for that option. For item 1, the probability of choosing at least *Sometimes* is 50% for those with failure avoidance = −3.08; the probability of choosing at least *Often* is 50% for those with failure avoidance = −.05; and the probability of choosing *Almost Always* is 50% for those with failure avoidance = 1.65. The metric of these values is set by the failure avoidance distribution. The average failure avoidance was set to 0, with a standard deviation of 1. The thresholds may be interpreted relative to this distribution.

The item parameters can also be interpreted graphically. For items 1 and 6, the probability of choosing each category or higher are shown in Figures 4.23 and 4.24 as a function of failure

(*continued*)

(*continued*)

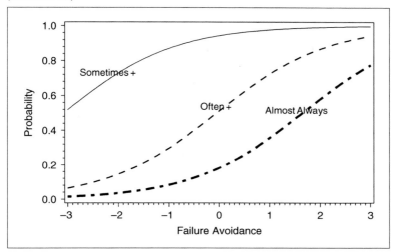

Figure 4.23. Probability of choosing each option or higher, Item 1.

avoidance. Similar graphs are shown for other items in the Appendix. The functions increase more steeply for item 6 because the discrimination is higher.

The category thresholds are well spread across the failure avoidance range. Within each item, the distance between the highest and lowest threshold is 2.6–4.7 units. Notice in Figures 4.23 and 4.24, the categories are spaced closer together for item 6 than for item 1. The categories are closer together for item 6 than for the other items, but are spread reasonably far apart even for this item. There are somewhat more thresholds above the midpoint of the failure avoidance range, so this scale will measure higher failure avoidance levels particularly well.

All of the standard errors are reasonably small. The item parameters are estimated with good precision.

The score distribution was estimated (using 20 quadrature points) along with the item parameters, on the same metric as the item parameters. The metric was set such that the mean failure avoidance level was 0 with a standard deviation of 1. A graph of the estimated distributed is available in Figure 4.25.

(*continued*)

(*continued*)

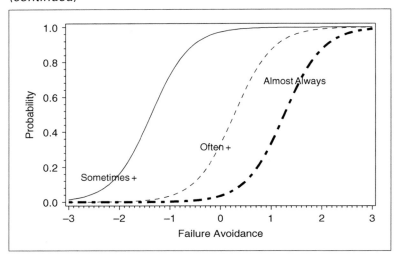

Figure 4.24. Probability of choosing each option or higher, Item 6.

Although the distribution is not exactly normal, the students are concentrated toward the middle of the continuum. The distribution is somewhat bimodal, with the largest mode just below the mean and a smaller mode above the mean, near 1.

A score on the motive to avoid failure scale was estimated for each respondent as well. Bayesian (expected a posterior) scoring was used, with a normal prior applied to the likelihood. This pulled extremely high or low scores in slightly toward more realistic levels. Bayesian scoring also provides more information for extreme scores than maximum likelihood scoring. It is important to know how precisely the failure avoidance scores are estimated. The information function indicates the precision of the failure avoidance estimates. The standard error of the failure avoidance score can be approximated by the square root of the inverse of the information function. The information function and standard error are plotted in Figure 4.26. Notice that there is more information/smaller standard errors just above the middle ranges of motivation to avoid failure, with a smaller peak near −1. This is

(*continued*)

(*continued*)

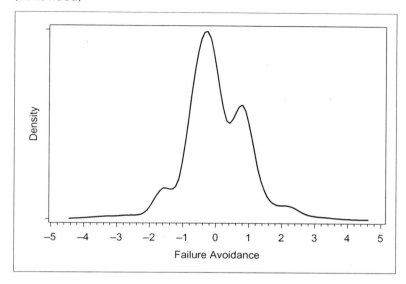

Figure 4.25. Estimated distribution of motivation to avoid failure.

because the information function is the sum of the item information functions. Each item gives more information near (although not precisely at) its thresholds. Because there were more thresholds just above the mean, there is more information in that range. Also, items with higher discrimination indices give more information. In Figure 4.27, the information function is plotted for item 6 (corresponding to the characteristic curve in Figure 4.24). The solid line shows the item information, and the dotted lines show the response category information functions, which sum to the item information. Information functions for other items are provided in the Appendix.

Standard errors, as shown in Figure 4.26, are useful for understanding the precision of a respondent's score. To summarize the precision with which examinees' scores can be differentiated, an average index of reliability can calculated. For Bayesian scores, the reliability can be calculated as: 1 − (error variance)/(observed variance + error variance), with the average squared standard error used for the error variance. For this group, the average reliability was .89. In comparison, the estimated

(*continued*)

(*continued*)

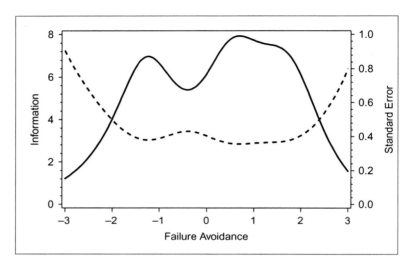

Figure 4.26. Test information and standard error of measurement.

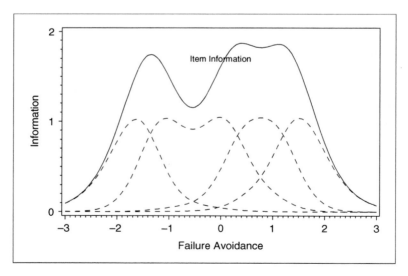

Figure 4.27. Item category information. The item information function is the sum of the item category information functions.

(*continued*)

(*continued*)

reliability of the raw scores was .84; the IRT scores were somewhat more reliable because IRT scoring takes into account the differential discrimination and category spacings of the items.

Comments on the Write-Up

Like the dichotomous write-up, this sample write-up referred to an appendix with additional figures, which was omitted to save space and because it would be of little interest except to the test developers or reviewers.

There were not enough items to run a statistical test of unidimensionality in POLY-DIMTEST because six items cannot reasonably be divided into an Assessment Subtest and a Partitioning Subtest. Instead, the eigenvalues of the correlation matrix were computed for a sense of whether unidimensionality was tenable, as discussed in Chapter 3 (this volume). Although less definitive, this provides some check on the assumption. This method is based on a linear model, but as the number of categories per item increases, linear models approximate ordinal item scores with increasing accuracy if the response distribution is reasonably normal (Bollen, 1989, Chapter 9; Finney & DiStefano, 2006). Examination of the eigenvalues provides only a rough check on unidimensionality, and the results should not be overinterpreted. Multivariate item response models (equivalently known as *full-information factor analysis models*) would be more appropriate for a more extensive study of dimensionality. Factor analysis of the polychoric correlation matrix is another advanced analysis method that often gives results similar to full-information factor analysis (see Finney & DiStefano, 2006, for a discussion of appropriate estimation methods and software for analysis of polychoric correlations).

Maximum likelihood scores were used in the dichotomous example, and EAP scores were used in the polytomous example to provide a sample write-up of each. Unfortunately, Bayesian scores require a bit more explanation. If the standard deviation of the score estimates (as opposed to the estimated standard deviation) had been presented in the example, it would have been smaller than 1. As explained in the beginning of the chapter, the Bayesian scores are shrunken inward, and thus the standard deviation of the θ estimates is less than the direct estimate of the standard deviation. Typically, the metric is set based on the direct estimate of the population distribution, although it could optionally be based on the distribution of the θ estimates instead. Also, this write-up stated that the Bayesian information function (which includes the prior distribution) can be used to approximate the standard errors. Recall that this is only an approximation. The Bayesian information function is the inverse of the squared standard error for the MAP scores, not the EAP scores. This seemed a bit too much detail for this illustration.

Figure 4.22 in this example could have shown the residuals for the proportions in each category instead of the residual for the expected item score. An example was shown in Chapter 3 in Figure 3.4 (in this volume). This would have corresponded to the residuals used in calculating G^2. Although this figure would provide more information, it would also be more difficult for the reader to integrate and interpret that information, particularly with larger numbers of response options or scoring categories.

The threshold parameters in Table 4.2 for this GR model could have been separated into the location and category parameters. The parameters and an explanation of these parameters (omitting the explanation of the a-parameter because it is unchanged) would have been:

Table 4.3

Decomposed Graded Response (GR) Parameters

Item	Slope	SE	Location	SE	c_1	SE	c_2	SE	c_3	SE
1	0.75	0.02	−0.49	0.03	2.59	0.08	−0.44	0.03	−2.14	0.05
2	1.16	0.02	−0.31	0.02	1.74	0.05	−0.19	0.02	−1.55	0.03
3	1.05	0.02	0.53	0.02	2.00	0.04	−0.28	0.03	−1.72	0.05
4	1.41	0.03	0.67	0.02	1.47	0.02	−0.15	0.02	−1.33	0.04
5	1.76	0.04	0.35	0.02	1.63	0.03	−0.22	0.02	−1.41	0.04
6	1.54	0.03	0.05	0.02	1.42	0.03	−0.22	0.02	−1.21	0.03

(continued)

(*continued*)

The item location is the mean of the thresholds and indicates the overall difficulty of the item. Item 1 was the easiest to endorse, and item 4 was the most difficult. To find the point on the Motivation to Avoid Failure scale at which 50% of examinees choose a given category or higher, subtract the category parameter from the location. The resulting threshold indicates the score value at which 50% of respondents choose the designated option or higher. Everyone has a 100% probability of choosing Strongly Disagree or higher, so there is no threshold for that option. For item 1, the probability of choosing at least Disagree is 50% for those with failure avoidance $= -0.49 - 2.59 = -3.08$; the probability of choosing at least Agree is 50% for those with failure avoidance $= -0.49 - (-0.44) = -.05$; and the probability of choosing Strongly Agree is 50% for those with failure avoidance $= -0.49 - (-2.14) = 1.65$.

The advantage of separating the threshold parameters this way is that the item location summarizes the overall item difficulty. The disadvantage is that the category parameters must then be subtracted from the location to find the thresholds. Notice that the standard errors of the category parameters are smaller when the thresholds are decomposed, because the standard errors are also decomposed.

These items could have been calibrated with the GPC model instead of the GR. Primarily, this would change the meaning of the *b*-parameters, which would be step difficulties instead of thresholds. The *a*-parameters are lower in the GPC model when there are more than two categories, so with three or more categories, *a*-parameters from different models should not be compared. However, the basic interpretation of the *a*-parameter as an

The data were calibrated with a Generalized Partial Credit (GPC) model. The constant 1.7 was used in the model, so that the scale would approximate the normal metric. Table 4.4 shows the estimated item parameters. The slope is an index of how rapidly the response probability changes as failure-avoidance motivation

(*continued*)

(*continued*)

increases. The step difficulties (*b*-parameters) indicate the point on the failure avoidance scale at which two adjacent responses are equally likely. For example, at the first step difficulty *Almost Never* and *Sometimes* are equally likely; before the step difficulty *Almost Never* is more likely and after the step difficulty *Sometimes* is more likely. For item 1, the probabilities of *Almost Never* and *Sometimes* are equal at failure avoidance = −3.35; the probabilities of *Sometimes* and *Often* are equal at failure avoidance = 0.20; the probabilities of *Often* and *Almost Always* are equal at failure avoidance = 1.35.

Table 4.4

Generalized Partial Credit Model Parameters

Item	Slope	SE	Step 1	SE	Step 2	SE	Step 3	SE
1	0.57	0.02	−3.35	0.12	0.20	0.06	1.35	0.07
2	0.96	0.03	−2.08	0.06	−0.02	0.04	1.11	0.04
3	0.87	0.02	−1.54	0.05	0.93	0.04	1.94	0.07
4	1.21	0.04	−0.78	0.03	0.87	0.03	1.78	0.06
5	1.64	0.04	−1.27	0.03	0.61	0.03	1.61	0.04
6	1.33	0.04	−1.38	0.04	0.36	0.03	1.11	0.04

indicator of how much the response probability changes as a function of θ is the same. An example follows.

The write-up would then have continued in a manner similar to the write-up for the GR model, with details on fit, information, and so forth. As for the GR model, the step difficulties for the GPC model could have been separated into location and category parameters. The example would be similar, except that the category parameters would be used to calculate step difficulties instead of thresholds.

Chapter Summary

This chapter began with an explanation of how the item parameters and θs are estimated. The text that followed explained how each of the questions introduced in Chapter 2 (in this volume) could be answered. The examples in this chapter have shown some of the ways that the results could be described in a report. The next chapter provides examples of a brief discussion of the results.

Appendix

Technical Details

Maximum Likelihood Estimation of θ. The natural log of a function reaches its maximum at the same point at which the function reaches its maximum. In IRT, the log-likelihood is easier to work with than the likelihood because the log-likelihood is the sum of the log-likelihoods for the individual responses. Recall that the likelihood function is the product of the likelihoods for the individual responses. Sums are easier to compute than products, especially given that each likelihood is less than 1, so the product quickly gets very small. To find the maximum, we use the principle that a function reaches a maximum (at least a local maximum, relative to the nearby region) at the point where its first derivative is 0. Near this point, the second derivative is large, relative to the first derivative. So, if the derivatives of the log-likelihood functions are evaluated at a θ near the maximum, the ratio of the first derivative to the second derivative will be small. Also, in this close region, the signs of the derivatives will be the same if the estimate of θ is too high, and they will be opposite if the estimate of θ is too low. Thus, the ratio can be used to estimate how far off an estimate is and in which direction it should change. At the first step of the estimation, an initial guess for θ can be based on a transformation of the number-correct score. Or, it can simply be 0. For this value of θ, we find the ratio of the first derivative to the second derivative and update the estimate of θ by subtracting this ratio. If the previous estimate of θ was close to where the function would be maximized, θ will be updated by only a small amount. The first and second derivatives are then evaluated at the updated θ value. The process continues, or iterates between these steps, until the change in θ meets some specified stopping criteria, such as 0.01. At that point, the iterations are said to converge, because the value is nearly unchanged between iterations.

For Bayesian estimation, the likelihood is multiplied by the prior distribution of θ (usually based on the group's or subgroup's θ distribution). The product is rescaled to have a density of 1; this is the posterior distribution of θ (the posterior distribution for the individual examinee, or individual response pattern—not to be confused with the group-level posterior distribution resulting from the MML item calibration). For MAP estimation, the maximum (mode) of the posterior (or of the log of the posterior) is then found as described above for ML estimation. Finding the mean of the distribution, or the EAP estimate of θ, requires a different step. The posterior distribution is approximated using the method of quadratures. Along a plausible range of θ, perhaps –4 to 4, a series of points (quadrature points) are specified at equal intervals (they do not have to be at equal intervals—Gaussian quadrature points, for example, are spaced more tightly in the center where the normal density is higher—but for this discussion, we will use equal intervals for simplicity). In Figure 4.28, the points are spaced every 0.2 units. A rectangle can be envisioned, with width equal to 0.2 (0.1 on either side) and height equal to the value of the function. The mean (expected value) of θ can be found by taking a weighted average, weighting each quadrature point by the area of the rectangle drawn around that point (or simply the height, if the points are evenly spaced, so that all the widths are equal). For the distribution in Figure 4.28, Table 4.5 shows the calculations. The weights were scaled to sum to 1, so the weighted mean is the sum of θ times the weight. The EAP estimate for this examinee is 0.35. The

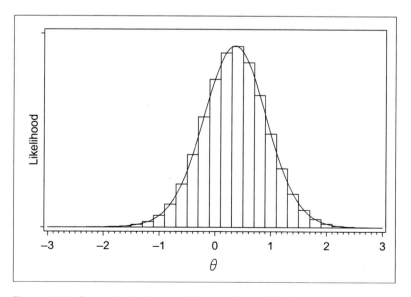

Figure 4.28. Posterior likelihood of θ, approximated by the method of quadratures.

Table 4.5

Expected A-Posterior Estimation

θ	Density (weight)	θ × weight
−3.0	0.00002	−0.00006
−2.6	0.00005	−0.00013
−2.2	0.00022	−0.00048
−1.8	0.00094	−0.00169
−1.4	0.00417	−0.00584
−1.0	0.01833	−0.01833
−0.6	0.06715	−0.04029
−0.2	0.17047	−0.03409
0.2	0.26984	0.05397
0.6	0.25504	0.15302
1.0	0.14538	0.14538
1.4	0.05269	0.07377
1.8	0.01300	0.02340
2.2	0.00233	0.00513
2.6	0.00032	0.00083
3.0	0.00003	0.00009
sum	1.00000	0.35467

standard deviation of the posterior can also be calculated from these value—this is the standard error of the EAP score.

Group Reliability Estimates

To calculate marginal reliability, Green and colleagues (1984) proposed integrating the squared standard error of measurement (from the information function) over the θ distribution. The reliability for the ML θ scores can then be calculated as:

$$\text{reliability} = \frac{s_\theta^2 - \bar{s}_e^2}{s_\theta^2},$$ where s_θ^2 is the variance of the score estimates

(in other words, the observed score variance) and $\bar{s}_e^2$ is the marginal (average) squared standard error. Because Rasch model users most commonly use ML scores, reliability of person separation is calculated using this formula, too (Bond & Fox, 2001, Chapter 3; Wilson, 2005, Chapter 7; Wright & Masters, 1982, Chapter 5). If the metric is standardized such that the variance of the score estimates, instead of the direct estimate of the variance of θ, is fixed to 1, then the reliability is more simply: $1 - \bar{s}_e^2$ (Thissen & Orlando, 2001, p. 119).

Similar indices are available in BILOG-MG (Zimowski, Muraki, Mislevy, & Bock, 2003, pp. 33–34). For the *empirical* reliability of ML scores, $\bar{s}_e^2$ for the formula above is calculated as the mean of the squared standard errors for the examinees in the sample. (More precisely, the mean of 1/(squared standard error) is calculated, and then $\bar{s}_e^2 = 1/$(this result). This value will be close to, but not precisely equal to, the mean of the squared standard errors). For the sample write-up of the history/political science test, $\bar{s}_e^2 = 0.1430$, and $s_{\hat{\theta}}^2 = 1.1135$. Reliability $= (1.1135 - 0.1430)/1.1135 = .872$, providing the value given in the example. The empirical reliability for Bayesian scores is calculated slightly differently, because the variance of the score estimates underestimates the θ variance. The reliability index for Bayesian scores in BILOG-MG is: reliability $=$ $\frac{s_{\hat{\theta}}^2}{s_{\hat{\theta}}^2 + \bar{s}_e^2}$. For the Bayesian scores for the sample data (not discussed in the write-up because ML scores were used there), $s_{\hat{\theta}}^2 = 0.8773$ and $\bar{s}_e^2 = 0.1401$. Reliability $= 0.8773/(0.8773 + 0.1401) = .862$. Mislevy, Beaton, Kaplan, and Sheehan (1992) showed a similar formula, substituting the direct estimate of the θ variance (usually 1) for the denominator. On average, this will be equivalent because the expected value (average over many samples) of the variance of the Bayesian score estimates plus the error variance $=$ the direct estimate of the variance. In other words, the Bayesian estimates are shrunken proportionally to their reliability. If the metric is scaled such that the direct estimate of the variance of $\theta = 1$, then the variance of the Bayesian score estimates is an estimate of the reliability.

For the *theoretical* reliability optionally reported in BILOG-MG, $\bar{s}_e^2$ is found by integrating the information function over a normal distribution of θ; $\bar{s}_e^2$ is then 1/mean information. The theoretical reliability index is: reliability $= \frac{1}{1+\bar{s}_e^2}$, because the true score variance is defined to be 1. When the direct estimate of the variance (estimated true score variance) of the θ distribution is fixed to 1, the calculated value of this index should be close to the value obtained from Green and colleagues' definition, because the expected value of the variance of the ML estimates = the variance of θ + error variance. For the data used in the sample write-up, $\bar{s}_e^2 = 0.1401$. The $\bar{s}_e^2$ used in the empirical reliability formula was a bit larger because of the non-normality of the θ distribution; the heavy left tail was in a region of low information. The theoretical reliability = $1/1.1401 = .877$. In summary, each of the estimation methods gives slightly different results in this sample, but the estimates are not far apart.

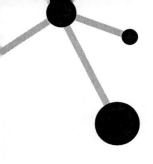

5

DISCUSSION

AS IN CHAPTER 4, the focus of this chapter is limited to a technical report or test development summary. These reports would be directed to the test development team or test users because they are focused on a particular test. They would not be designed to answer generalizable research questions that might interest journal readers or research conference attendees. The Discussion section for an item response theory (IRT) analysis should include recommendations about which items should be deleted/modified, and about appropriate uses of the instrument. The Discussion, like the Results, can be organized around the research questions.

Four of the questions should be considered together:

- What is the spread of item difficulties (and category difficulties, for polytomous items)?
- How discriminating is each item?
- What is the distribution of abilities/traits in this group of examinees/respondents? How does the ability distribution compare to the item difficulty distribution?
- How does each item contribute to the test information?

The difficulty of the items should be considered in relationship to the distribution of the θs in the population for which the instrument is intended. Difficulty (*b*-parameters) should be discussed in terms of information relative to the θ distribution. For many instruments, it is desirable to have items throughout the θ range where most examinees/participants are, perhaps –2 to 2 if the sample used to establish the scale metric is similar to the intended population. For some instruments, it might be important to have many items with *b*-parameters in a particular range. For example, if there is a cut-score, such as a passing standard or a value for clinical diagnosis, it is important to have high information near that score, so that θs near that value can be estimated with small standard errors. As detailed in Chapter 4 (in this volume), items reach their highest information at the location of the item difficulty or near the category thresholds or step difficulties. Thus, items should be clustered near the cut-score. However, this design limits the test use to discriminating between students close to the cut-score, while θs in other parts of the range may be estimated far less precisely. For example, a psychological well-being test for university students may initially be intended to identify students who have relatively low levels of well-being because they may benefit from additional student services. If the test is targeted to these students, it will not be as useful for monitoring minor changes in the well-being of most members of the student population. Even if students experience a drop in psychological well-being, most will still remain in the range where there are not enough items to detect the change. The test developers may have a broader market if they select a wider range of item difficulties. But the instrument may be more useful to a niche market if the *b*-parameters have a narrow range but provide very precise scores within that range. Licensure/certification tests, for example, are typically intended to determine whether the applicant has the competency to practice in a career field. They are not necessarily intended to differentiate among examinees at other levels.

As these examples show, the context must be carefully considered when recommending which items are of appropriate difficulty. If items are too easy or too difficult for the intended use, they will contribute little to the information for (reliability of) the scores. A test that is not well-matched to the intended examinee population will require many more items (and thus testing time and test-development costs) to achieve the same information (reliability) as a test well-matched to the population and intended use.

This discussion has focused on how the item difficulties, relative to the θ distribution, affect the measurement properties of the test scores. In addition, the item difficulties and θ distribution could be examined with a focus on content. Item maps could be used to illustrate which types of skills most examinees have mastered and which types of skills few examinees have mastered. Or, for a psychological trait or attitude, the item map would show which statements are endorsed by respondents at different levels of the trait.

Item discrimination (slope) should also be considered in the recommendations concerning which items are acceptable. If the probability of correct response (endorsement) is not much higher for examinees who have high θs than for those who have low θs, the item can not help measure θ very well. It might instead be measuring an uncorrelated construct or be poorly written. Low-discriminating items take testing time that could instead be used for more informative items (or for nontesting activities, such as instruction if the test is administered during school time). If the lack of discrimination is due to a confusing question or response options, examinees' performance on other test items could possibly be impacted. In short, items that do not discriminate well should seldom be left on the test. They should be referred back to a content committee or group of item writers for suggestions on whether each item should be rewritten or discarded.

How Much Information Does the Test Provide over the Ability/Trait Range?

Here the Discussion section moves from discussion/recommendations for individual items to discussion at the score level. The implications of the information function reported in the Results section can be explained. For example, does the test provide information throughout the θ distribution? If not, is this the result of an intentional instrument design decision, such as targeting a particular θ level, or does the test need more items in a particular θ range? This discussion might be tied to the consideration of item information as well.

For a Given Population or Sample Distribution, How Reliable Are the Ability/Trait Estimates?

The reliability estimate provided in the Results section should be interpreted relative to the intended test use. The guidelines commonly used for other reliability estimates, such as KR-20/coefficient α, can be used for the IRT-based marginal reliability as well. For example, Traub (1994, p. 39) noted that high-stakes educational tests typically have reliabilities at least in the .80s, although psychological/attitude scales sometimes have lower reliability. Roid (2006) recommended .80 as a minimum for subtest scores and .90 as a minimum for total scores. Buckendahl, Impara, and Plake (2002) suggested as low as .70 might be acceptable if the results were used only for group-level inferences, not for individual student inferences.

The following sample Discussion sections would accompany the Results sections in Chapter 4 (in this volume). The first example is for the multiple-choice U.S. history and political science test, and the second example is for the Motivation to Avoid Failure scale.

Discussion and Recommendations

Most of the item difficulties were in a reasonable range for productive measurement. A few items were so easy that they provided no information about what examinees know—items 12, 19, 20, and 38. These items might be useful if the test will be used with a less-knowledgeable population, such as a pre-test for students before they take the courses associated with the test. Otherwise, the time spent reading and responding to these items would be better utilized on more difficult items. Most of the item discriminations were adequate. More information could be obtained if items 2, 12, 31, 38, and 39 were replaced with more discriminating items. Of these items, 12 and 38 were also very easy.

The item difficulties (b's) shown in the Results indicated which items are typically challenging for the highest-proficiency students, which are challenging for middle-proficiency students but mastered by most higher-proficiency students, etc. From a psychometric perspective, these are simply empirical alignments

(*continued*)

(*continued*)

and not useful for recommendations. However, the course instructors and other content experts should examine these alignments to see if they are reasonable. If the instructors believe that a difficult item should be easier, they should consider how the item is worded. Is one of the distractors unnecessarily misleading? Is the question stem or the correct answer too confusing? If the instructors are surprised that an item is easier than expected based on the concept, they should make sure that no extraneous clues in the item made the correct answer too obvious. For example, the correct answer should not be considerably longer than the other options, and all options should be grammatically parallel. The distractors should appear reasonable to a student who has not learned the course material. Such flaws may be empirically detected if they lead to lower item discriminations, but content experts are needed to explore whether the empirical item difficulty is consistent with the predicted difficulty of the item content. Further, course instructors can consider whether the conflict between expectations and empirical difficulty might be due to course emphasis rather than flaws in the item. Such consideration might reveal information about how students learn; if students are missing foundational concepts that seem obvious to the instructors (and thus are not covered in the course), instructors might want to spend some initial time making sure students understand the basic concepts before they attempt to build on them.

The test information function shows that the test is reasonably informative for most examinees. It is more informative for middle-proficiency levels. Averaging across all examinees, the estimated reliability of .87 is acceptable for program assessment. Somewhat higher reliability would be desirable if the test had high stakes for individual students, such as a mandatory passing standard or assignment to further coursework. The test is fairly short, and adding more items would likely increase the reliability (assuming the additional items measured the same construct). This is not needed for the current use of the test scores, and given that the test is currently given in low-stakes conditions it is probably better to keep it short to better maintain the attention of the examinees.

In the first paragraph of the write-up, it was noted that two of the less-discriminating items were also quite easy. Sometimes it can be difficult to estimate the a-parameters for very easy or difficult items. The standard errors for the a-parameters for these items were not unusually large, though, so it does not seem to have been a problem here and thus was not mentioned in the write-up.

In this write-up, references were made to the course instructors and to the course grades. For many standardized tests, the content is not geared toward a particular course and *content experts* would be substituted for *course instructors*. Committees of content experts, such as experienced teachers (for a K–12 test) or faculty and employers (for a certification/licensure exam) or counselors (for a psychological survey) are typically convened by test-development companies at various points throughout the test development. Similarly, the context of the test administration and use of the scores was an important consideration in the Discussion. These will, of course, vary, so recommendations need to take context into account.

The next example is a follow-up to the Results section for the failure-avoidance motivation scale.

Discussion and Recommendations

For each of these items, the response scale covered a reasonable spread of the failure avoidance continuum for this group of respondents.

Experts on motivation to avoid failure should examine the locations of the items to ensure that the items are ordered consistently with definitions of the construct. If any item seems empirically mis-ordered, the item should be examined for clarity.

Each of the items had reasonable discrimination and provided information about the degree to which the respondent was motivated to avoid failure. While item 1 had the lowest slope, it made the greatest contribution to information at the lowest levels of the failure avoidance motivation continuum because it had the lowest threshold.

The information covered the failure avoidance motivation spectrum for this population well. The overall reliability, averaged over all failure avoidance levels, was .89. This is quite good for such a short instrument.

In this write-up, there was less to say than in the multiple-choice write-up because the results were good. Recommendations for removal of items or addition of new items would of course have been made if such recommendations were warranted. The a-parameter for item 1 might have been considered a bit low for dichotomous items, but when combined with dispersed thresholds within the item, as in this example, a polytomous item with a lower a-parameter can still provide substantial information. Thus, these a-parameters were not highlighted in the Discussion.

Chapter Summary

This chapter described how the findings in the Results could be summarized, discussed, and used for further recommendations. The context of the test administration, the examinee population, and the use of the scores are important considerations in the Discussion. The sample write-ups gave examples in two particular contexts. This chapter concludes the text. The next chapter will provide some suggestions for further reading.

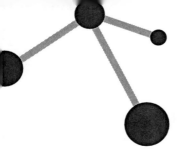

6

ADDITIONAL READING

FOR MORE advanced general information on item response theory (IRT) that is fairly easy to understand, consider R.J. de Ayala's *The Theory and Practice of Item Response Theory* (New York: Guilford Press, 2009). This book provides an excellent balance of conceptual explanations and mathematical detail. In addition to explaining various IRT models and estimation procedures, it presents introductions to equating, differential item functioning, and computerized adaptive testing.

R.K. Hambleton, H. Swaminathan, and H.J. Rogers's *Fundamentals of Item Response Theory* (Newbury Park, CA: Sage, 1991) provides introductions to differential item functioning, scaling/equating, and computerized adaptive testing. These applications show the advantages of IRT. A related text with somewhat more detail is R.K. Hambleton and H. Swaminathan's *Item Response Theory: Principles and Applications* (Boston: Kluwer, 1985).

Another comprehensive IRT text is S.E. Embretson and S.P. Reise's *Item Response Theory for Psychologists* (Mahwah, NJ: Lawrence Erlbaum Associates, 2000).

A good on-line introduction to IRT is found in F.B. Baker's *The Basics of Item Response Theory*, ERIC Clearinghouse on Assessment and Evaluation (2001). Available at http://edres.org/irt/.

There is also a very clear introduction to IRT in Chapter 3 (pp. 24–43) of H. Wainer, E.T. Bradlow, and X. Wang's *Testlet Response Theory and Its Applications* (New York: Cambridge University Press, 2007). This text contains much more advanced material on more complex models, but the first chapters are introductory. Chapter 3 contains a brief but lucid explanation of estimation procedures.

An easy-to-read comparison of polytomous models is available in R.J. de Ayala's article (1993) "An introduction to polytomous item response theory models" (*Measurement and Evaluation in Counseling and Development, 25,* 172–189.)

The current text only briefly touched on Rasch modeling. Two comprehendible books on Rasch modeling are M. Wilson's *Constructing Measures: An Item Response Modeling Approach* (Mahwah, NJ: Lawrence Erlbaum Associates, 2005); and T.G. Bond and C.M. Fox's *Applying the Rasch Model: Fundamental Measurement in the Human Sciences* (Mahwah, NJ: Lawrence Erlbaum Associates, 2001). Both of these books explain the philosophy of Rasch modeling and how it can be used throughout the test development process.

Rasch-modeling users should also consider E.V. and R.M. Smith's edited text, *Introduction to Rasch Measurement: Theory, Models, and Applications* (Maple Grove, MN: JAM Press, 2004). In particular, the chapters by Wilson and by Schumacker provide basic explanations and examples. Some of the other chapters provide more advanced models and applications.

A variety of different IRT-related software is described at: http://www.umass.edu/remp/remp_software.htm.

This book introduced only the most commonly used IRT models. Many more models are described by various authors in W.J. van der Linden and R.K. Hambleton's edited text *Handbook of Modern Item Response Theory* (New York: Springer, 1997).

Before attempting such an advanced book, readers will want to study some of the more basic texts listed above.

REFERENCES

American Educational Research Association, American Psychological Association, & National Council on Measurement in Education. (1999). *Standards for educational and psychological testing*. Washington, DC: American Educational Research Association.

Andrich, D. (1978). Application of a psychometric rating model to ordered categories which are scored with successive integers. *Applied Psychological Measurement, 2*, 581–594.

Andrich, D. (2002). Understanding resistance to the data-model relationship in Rasch's paradigm: A reflection for the next generation. *Journal of Applied Measurement, 3*, 325–359.

Baker, F. B., & Kim, S.-H. (2004). *Item response theory parameter estimation techniques* (2nd ed.). New York: Marcel Dekker.

Barnes, L. L. B., & Wise, S. L. (1991). The utility of a modified one-parameter IRT model with small samples. *Applied Measurement in Education, 4*, 143–157.

Beretvas, S. N. (2004). Comparison of Bookmark difficulty locations under different item response models. *Applied Psychological Measurement, 28*, 25–47.

Bock, R. D. (1972). Estimating item parameters and latent ability when responses are scored in two or more nominal categories. *Psychometrika, 37*, 29–51.

Bock, R. D., & Aitkin, M. (1981). Marginal maximum likelihood estimation of item parameters: Application of an EM algorithm. *Psychometrika, 46*, 443–459.

Bollen, K. A. (1989). *Structural equations with latent variables*. New York: John Wiley and Sons.

Bolt, D. M. (2002). A Monte-Carlo comparison of parametric and nonparametric polytomous DIF detection methods. *Applied Measurement in Education, 15*, 113–141.

Bond, T. G., & Fox, C. M. (2001). *Applying the Rasch model: Fundamental measurement in the human sciences*. Mahwah, NJ: Lawrence Erlbaum Associates.

Buckendahl, C. W., Impara, J. C., & Plake, B. S. (2002). District accountability without a state assessment: A proposed model. *Educational measurement: Issues and Practice, 21* (4), 6–16.

Chen, W-H., & Thissen, D. (1997). Local dependence indexes for item pairs using item response theory. *Journal of Educational and Behavioral Statistics, 22,* 265–289.

Choi, S. W., Cook, K. F., & Dodd, B. G. (1997). Parameter recovery for the partial credit model using MULTILOG. *Journal of Outcome Measurement, 1,* 114–142.

Cook, L. L., Eignor, D. R., & Taft, H. L. (1988). A comparative study of the effects of recency of instruction on the stability of IRT and conventional item parameter estimates. *Journal of Educational Measurement, 25,* 31–45.

de Ayala, R. J. (1993). An introduction to polytomous item response theory models. *Measurement and Evaluation in Counseling and Development, 25,* 172–189.

de Ayala, R. J., & Hertzog, M. A. (1991). The assessment of dimensionality for use in item response theory. *Multivariate Behavioral Research, 26,* 765–792.

de Ayala, R. J., & Sava-Bolesta, M. (1999). Item parameter recovery for the nominal response model. *Applied Psychological Measurement, 23,* 3–19.

De Champlain, A. F. (1999). Assessing the dimensionality of simulated LSAT item response matrices with small sample sizes and short test lengths. (Report No. LSAC-96-01). Princeton, NJ: Law School Admissions Council (ERIC Document Reproduction Service No ED467805)

De Champlain, A., & Gessaroli, M. E. (1998). Assessing the dimensionality of item response matrices with small sample sizes and short test lengths. *Applied Measurement in Education, 11,* 231–253.

DeMars, C. E. (2003a). Sample size and the recovery of nominal response model item parameters. *Applied Psychological Measurement, 27,* 275–288.

DeMars, C. E. (2003b). Detecting multidimensionality due to curricular differences. *Journal of Educational Measurement, 40,* 29–51.

DeMars, C. E. (2005). Type I error rates for PARSCALE's fit index. *Educational and Psychological Measurement, 65,* 42–50.

Donoghue, J. R., & Humbo, C. M. (2003, April). *A corrected asymptotic distribution of an IRT fit measure that accounts for the effects of item parameter estimation.* Paper presented at the annual meeting of the American Educational Research Association, Chicago.

Douglas, J., & Cohen, A. (2001). Nonparametric item response function estimation for assessing parametric model fit. *Applied Psychological Measurement, 25,* 234–243.

Dragow, F. (1989). An evaluation of marginal maximum likelihood estimation for the two-parameter logistic model. *Applied Psychological Measurement, 13,* 77–90.

Dragow, F., & Lissak, R. I. (1983). Modified parallel analysis: A procedure for examining the latent dimensionality of dichotomously scored item responses. *Journal of Applied Psychology, 68,* 363–373.

Embretson, S. E., & Reise, S. P. (2000). *Item response theory for psychologists.* Mahwah, NJ: Lawrence Erlbaum Associates.

Engelhard, G., Jr. (1992). The measurement of writing ability with a many-faceted Rasch model. *Applied Measurement in Education, 5,* 171–191.

Fan, X. (1998). Item response theory and classical test theory: An empirical comparison of their item/person statistics. *Educational and Psychological Measurement, 58,* 357–381.

Feldt, L. S., & Brennan, R. L. (1989). Reliability. In R. L. Linn (Ed.), *Educational Measurement* (3rd ed., pp. 105–146). Phoenix, AZ: American Council on Education/Oryx Press.

Finch, H., & Habing, B. (2007). Performance of DIMTEST- and NOHARM-based statistics for testing unidimensionality. *Applied Psychological Measurement, 31,* 292–307.

Finney, S. J., and DiStefano, C. (2006). Non-normal and categorical data in structural equation modeling. In G. R. Hancock and R. O. Mueller (Eds.), *Structural Equation Modeling: A Second Course* (pp. 269–314). Greenwich, CT: Information Age Publishing.

Fraser, C., & McDonald, R. P. (2003). *NOHARM 3.0.* Available at: http://people. niagaracollege.ca/cfraser/download/

Gao, F., & Chen, L. (2005). Bayesian or non-Bayesian: A comparison study of item parameter estimation in the three-parameter logistic model. *Applied Measurement in Education, 18,* 351–380.

Gessaroli, M. E., & De Champlain, A. F. (1996). Using an approximate chi-square statistic to test the number of dimensions underlying the responses to a set of items. *Journal of Educational Measurement, 33,* 157–179.

Glas, C. A. W., & Suárez Falcón, J. C. (2003). A comparison of item-fit statistics for the three-parameter logistic model. *Applied Psychological Measurement, 27,* 87–106.

Green, B. F., Bock, R. D., Humphreys, L. G., Linn, R. B., & Reckase, M. D. (1984). Technical guidelines for assessing computerized adaptive tests. *Journal of Educational Measurement, 21,* 347–360.

Hagtvet, K. A., & Benson, J. (1997). The motive to avoid failure and test anxiety responses: Empirical support for integration of two research traditions. *Anxiety, Stress, and Coping, 10,* 35–57.

Hambleton, R. K., & Rovinelli, R. J. (1986). Assessing the dimensionality of a set of test items. *Applied Psychological Measurement, 10,* 287–302.

Harwell, M. R., & Janosky, J. E. (1991). An empirical study of the effects of small datasets and varying prior variances on item parameter estimation in BILOG. *Applied Psychological Measurement, 15,* 279–291.

Hattie, J. (1984). An empirical study of various indices for determining unidimensionality. *Multivariate Behavioral Research, 19,* 49–78.

Hattie, J., Krakowski, K., Rogers, H. J., & Swaminathan, H. (1996). An assessment of Stout's index of essential unidimensionality. *Applied Psychological Measurement, 20,* 1–14.

Hulin, C. L., Lissak, R. I., & Drasgow, F. (1982). Recovery of two- and three-parameter logistic item characteristic curves: A Monte Carlo study. *Applied Psychological Measurement, 20,* 249–260.

Kang, T., & Chen, T. T. (2008). Performance of the generalized S-X^2 item fit index for polytomous IRT models. *Journal of Educational Measurement, 45*, 391–406.

Kang, T., Cohen, A. S., & Sung, H. J. (2005, April). *IRT model selection methods for polytomous items*. Paper presented at the annual meeting of the National Council on Measurement in Education, Montreal.

Kang, T., & Cohen, A. S. (2007). IRT model selection methods for dichotomous items. *Applied Psychological Measurement, 31*, 331–358.

Karabatsos, G. (2003). Comparing the aberrant response detection performance of thirty-six person fit statistics. *Applied Measurement in Education, 16*, 277–298.

Karantonis, A., & Sireci, S. G. (2006). The Bookmark standard-setting method: A literature review. *Educational Measurement: Issues and Practice, 25* (1) 4–12.

Li, S.,& Wells, C. S. (2006, April). *A model fit statistic for Samejima's Graded Response model*. Paper presented at the annual meeting of the National Council on Measurement in Education, San Francisco.

Liang, T., & Wells, C. S. (2007, April). *A model fit statistic for generalized partial credit model*. Paper presented at the annual meeting of the National Council on Measurement in Education, Chicago.

Linacre, J. M. (2006). *A user's guide to WINSTEPS and MINISTEPS Rasch-Model computer programs*. Chicago: Winsteps.com.

Lord, F. M. (1968). An analysis of the verbal scholastic aptitude test using Birnbaum's three-parameter logistic model. *Educational and Psychological Measurement, 28*, 989–1020,

Lord, F. M. (1974). Estimation of latent ability and item parameters when there are omitted responses. *Psychometrika, 39*, 247–264.

Lord, F. M. (1980). *Applications of item response theory to practical testing problems*. Hillsdale, NJ: Lawrence Erlbaum Associates.

Masters, G. N. (1982). A Rasch model for partial credit scoring. *Psychometrika, 47*, 149–174.

Maydeu-Olivares, A. (2001). Multidimensional item response theory modeling of binary data: Large sample properties of NOHARM estimates. *Journal of Educational and Behavioral Statistics, 26*, 51–71.

Maydeu-Olivares, A., Drasgow, F., & Mead, A. D. (1994). Distinguishing among parametric item response models for polychotomous ordered data. *Applied Psychological Measurement, 18*, 245–256.

Mislevy, R. J. (1984). Estimating latent distributions. *Psychometrika, 49*, 359–381.

Mislevy, R. J. (1986). Bayes modal estimation in item response models. *Psychometrika, 51*, 177–195.

Mislevy, R. J., Beaton, A. E., Kaplan, B., & Sheehan, K. M. (1992). Estimating population characteristics from sparse matrix samples of item responses. *Journal of Educational Measurement, 29*, 133–161.

Muraki, E. (1990). Fitting a polytomous item response model to Likert-type data. *Applied Psychological Measurement, 14*, 59–71.

Muraki, E. (1992). A generalized partial credit model: Application of an EM algorithm. *Applied Psychological Measurement, 16*, 159–176.

Muraki, E., & Bock, D. (2003). PARSCALE 4.0 [Computer software and manual]. Lincolnwood, IL: Scientific Software International.

Nandakumar, R., & Stout, W. (1993). Refinements of Stout's procedure for assessing latent trait unidimensionality. *Journal of Educational Statistics, 18,* 41–68.

Orlando, M., & Thissen, D. (2000). Likelihood-based item-fit indices for dichotomous item response theory models. *Applied Psychological Measurement, 24,* 50–64.

Orlando, M., & Thissen, D. (2003). Further investigation of the performance of $S-X^2$: An item fit index for use with dichotomous item response theory models. *Applied Psychological Measurement, 27,* 289–298.

Oshima, T. C., & Morris, S. B. (2008). An NCME instructional module on Raju's differential functioning of items and tests (DFIT). *Educational Measurement: Issues and Practice, 27* (3), 43–50.

Parshall, C. G., Kromrey, J. D., Chason, W. M., & Yi, Q. (1997, June). *Evaluation of parameter estimation under modified IRT models and small samples.* Paper presented at the annual meeting of the Psychometric Society, Gatlinburg, TN. (ERIC Document Reproduction Service No ED421535)

Patz, R. J., & Junker, B. W. (1999). Applications and extensions of MCMC in IRT: Multiple item types, missing data, and rated responses. *Journal of Educational and Behavioral Statistics, 24,* 342–366.

Rasch, G. (1980). *Probabilistic models for some intelligence and attainment tests* (Exp. ed.). Chicago: University of Chicago Press. (Original work published 1960, Copenhagen: Danish Institute for Educational Research)

Reckase, M. D. (1979). Unifactor latent trait models applied to multifactor tests: Results and implications. *Journal of Educational Statistics, 4,* 207–230.

Reckase, M. D., Ackerman, T. A., & Carlson, J. E. (1988). Building a unidimensional test using multidimensional items. *Journal of Educational Measurement, 25,* 193–203.

Reise, S. P. (1990). A comparison of item- and person-fit methods of assessing model-data fit in IRT. *Applied Psychological Measurement, 14,* 127–137.

Reise, S. P., & Yu, J. (1990). Parameter recovery in the graded response model using MULTILOG. *Journal of Educational Measurement, 27,* 133–144.

Roid, G. H. (2006). Designing ability tests. In S. M. Downing & T. M. Haladyna, *Handbook of Test Development* (pp. 527–542). Mahwah, NJ: LEA.

Samejima, F. (1969). Estimation of latent ability using a response pattern of graded scores. *Psychometrika Monograph Supplements, 17.*

Sass, D. A., Schmitt, T. A., & Walker, C. M. (2008). Estimating non-normal latent trait distributions within item response theory using true and estimated item parameters. *Applied Measurement in Education, 21,* 65–88.

Schumacker, R. E. (2004). Rasch measurement: The dichotomous model. In E. V. Smith, Jr., & R. M. Smith (Eds.), *Introduction to Rasch measurement: Theory, models, and applications* (pp. 226–257). Maple Grove, MN: JAM Press.

Sijtsma, K., & Meijer, R. R. (2007). Nonparametric item response theory and special topics. In C. R. Rao & S. Sinharary (Eds.), *Handbook of Statistics, Vol. 26: Psychometrics* (pp. 719–746). Amsterdam: Elsevier.

Sinharay, S., & Lu, Y. (2008). A further look at the correlation between item parameters and item fit statistics. *Journal of Educational Measurement, 45,* 1–15.

Sireci, S. G., Thissen, D., & Wainer, H. (1991). On the reliability of testlet-based tests. *Journal of Educational Measurement, 28,* 237–247.

Smith, R. M., Schumacker, R. E., and Bush, M. J. (1998). Using item mean squares to evaluate fit to the Rasch model. *Journal of Outcome Measurement, 2,* 66–78.

Stone, C. A. (1992). Recovery of marginal maximum likelihood estimates in the two-parameter logistic response model: An evaluation of MULTILOG. *Applied Psychological Measurement, 16,* 1–16.

Stone, C. A. (2000). Monte Carlo based null distribution for an alternative goodness-of-fit test statistic in IRT models. *Journal of Educational Measurement, 37,* 58–75.

Stone, C. A. (2003). Empirical power and Type I error rates for an IRT fit statistic that considers the precision of ability estimates. *Educational and Psychological Measurement, 63,* 566–583.

Stone, C. A., & Hansen, M. A. (2000). The effect of errors in estimating ability on goodness-of-fit tests for IRT models. *Educational and Psychological Measurement, 60,* 974–991.

Stout, W. (1987). A nonparametric approach for assessing latent trait unidimensionality. *Psychometrika, 52,* 589–617.

Stout, W. (1999). Poly-DIMTEST [Computer software]. Champaign, IL: The William Stout Institute for Measurement.

Stout, W. (2005). DIMTEST (Version 2.0) [Computer software]. Champaign, IL: The William Stout Institute for Measurement.

Swaminathan, H., Hambleton, R. K., & Rogers, H. J. (2007). Assessing the fit of item response theory models. In C. R. Rao & S. Sinharay (Eds.), *Handbook of Statistics, Vol. 26: Psychometrics* (pp. 683–718). Amsterdam: Elsevier.

Tate, R. (2003). A comparison of selected empirical methods for assessing the structure of responses to test items. *Applied Psychological Measurement, 27,* 159–203.

Thissen, D., & Orlando, M. (2001). Item response theory for items scored in two categories. In D. Thissen & H. Wainer (Eds.), *Test Scoring* (pp. 73–140). Mahwah, NJ: Lawrence Erlbaum.

Thissen, D., Steinberg, L, & Gerrard, M. (1986). Beyond group differences: The concept of item bias. *Psychological Bulletin, 99,* 118–128.

Traub, R. E. (1994). *Reliability for the Social Sciences.* Newbury Park, CA: Sage.

Wainer, H., Bradlow, E. T., & Wang, X. (2007). *Testlet response theory and its applications.* New York: Cambridge University Press.

Wainer, H., & Wang, X. (2000). Using a new statistical model for testlets to score TOEFL. *Journal of Educational Measurement, 37,* 203–220.

Weiss, D. J. (1983). Polychotomous or polytomous? *Applied Psychological Measurement, 7,* 4.

Wells, C. S., & Bolt, D. M. (2008). Investigation of a nonparametric procedure for assessing goodness-of-fit item response theory. *Applied Measurement in Education, 21,* 22–40.

Wilson, M. (2004). On choosing a model for measuring. In E. V. Smith, Jr., & R. M. Smith (Eds.), *Introduction to Rasch Measurement: Theory, Models, and Applications* (pp. 123–142). Maple Grove, MN: JAM Press.

Wilson, M. (2005). *Constructing measures: An item response modeling approach.* Mahwah, NJ: Lawrence Erlbaum Associates.

Wingersky, M. S. (1983). LOGIST: A program for computing maximum likelihood procedures for logistic test models. In R. K. Hambleton (Ed.), *Applications of Item Response Theory* (pp. 45–56). British Columbia: Educational Research Institute of British Columbia.

Wolf, L. F., & Smith, J. K. (1995). The consequence of consequence: Motivation, anxiety, and test performance. *Applied Measurement in Education, 8,* 227–242.

Woods, C. M. (2006). Ramsay-curve item response theory to detect and correct for nonnormal latent variables. *Psychological Methods, 11,* 253–270.

Woods, C. M. (2008a). Consequences of ignoring guessing when estimating the latent density in item response theory. *Applied Psychological Measurement, 32,* 371–384.

Woods, C. M. (2008b). Ramsay-curve item response theory for the three-parameter-logistic item response model. *Applied Psychological Measurement, 32,* 447–465.

Wright, B. D., & Linacre, J. M. (1994). Reasonable mean-square fit values. *Rasch Measurement Transactions, 8,* 370.

Wright, B. D. (1997). A history of social science measurement. *Educational Measurement: Issues and Practice, 16* (4) 33–45, 52.

Wright, B. D., & Masters, G. N. (1982). *Rating scale analysis.* Chicago: MESA Press.

Wright, B. D., & Stone, M. (1979). *Best test design.* Chicago: MESA Press.

Yen, W. M. (1981). Using simulation results to choose a latent trait model. *Applied Psychological Measurement, 5,* 245–262.

Yen, W. M. (1984). Effects of local item dependence on the fit and equating performance of the three-parameter logistic model. *Applied Psychological Measurement, 8,* 125–145.

Yen, W. M. (1993). Scaling performance assessments: Strategies for managing local item dependence. *Journal of Educational Measurement, 30,* 187–213.

Zimowski, M., Muraki, E., Mislevy, R., & Bock, D. (2003). BILOG-MG [Computer software and manual]. Lincolnwood, IL: Scientific Software International.

Zwick, R., Senturk, D., Wang, J., & Loomis, S. C. (2001). An investigation of alternative methods for item mapping in the National Assessment of Educational Progress. *Educational Measurement: Issues and Practice, 20* (2), 15–25.

Zwick, W. R., & Velicer, W. F. (1986). Comparison of five rules for determining the number of components to retain. *Psychological Bulletin, 99,* 432–442.

INDEX

CPSIA information can be obtained at www.ICGtesting.com
Printed in the USA
BVOW02s0010190515

400670BV00005B/38/P